PSYCHOLOGY
in Practice

Education

Merv Stapleton

Series Editor: Hugh Coolican

Hodder & Stoughton

A MEMBER OF THE HODDER HEADLINE GROUP

This book is dedicated to Linda, Sian and Laura.

Thank you for all your love, support, encouragement and understanding. I could not have written this book without it. The takeaway is on me!!

Thanks also to Jane Roberts, for her shining example of how to be a quality teacher, Jude Letham and Susan Watt for their encouragement and support during my early years in teaching and Jacky Owen for her support and encouragement during the writing of this book.

Finally, thanks to all the students I have taught over the last ten years, many of whom a lot of the material in this book was 'road-tested' on (special mention to Amy Warhurst for her comments on some of the chapters!)...it was sometimes a pleasure, sometimes a privilege, but always a challenge!!

Merv Stapleton
Sunderland
July 2001

The publishers would like to thank G. I. Bernard/Oxford Scientific Films for permission to reproduce Figure 4.4

Orders: please contact Bookpoint Ltd, 130 Milton Park, Abingdon, Oxon OX14 4SB. Telephone: (44) 01235 827720. Fax: (44) 01235 400454. Lines are open from 9.00 – 6.00, Monday to Saturday, with a 24 hour message answering service. Email address: orders@bookpoint.co.uk

British Library Cataloguing in Publication Data
A catalogue record for this title is available from the British Library

ISBN 0 340 64329 3

First Published 2001
Impression number   10 9 8 7 6 5 4 3 2 1
Year   2007 2006 2005 2004 2003 2002 2001

Typeset by Dorchester Typesetting Group Limited, Dorset, England
Printed in Great Britain for Hodder & Stoughton Educational, a division of Hodder Headline Plc, 338 Euston Road, London NW1 3BH by The Bath Press Ltd.

CONTENTS

Introduction

Education! Education!! Education!!!

Given the amount of time that politicians spend talking about it, the amount of money spent on it, and last, but not least, the amount of time you spend 'consuming' it, it seems obvious that education is an important topic.

From your own experiences you will be very much aware of the complexities of the world of education. You will undoubtedly have had both positive and negative experiences during your educational career. You will have been taught by some good teachers and, some (but hopefully, not many!) not so good teachers. You will have passed examinations and, maybe, failed to pass some, at least at the first attempt. This experience means that you are already experts in the field of education. You have, after all been partaking of it since you were four or five years old!

Your experience and understanding of education, however, has largely been restricted to the perspective of a student. There is far more involved in education than sitting in a classroom and being taught. How do you learn? Why do different teachers teach in different ways? Why are some students keen and eager to learn, whilst others are thinking about what they're going to have for tea? Why do some teachers kick up a fuss if you so much as whisper to your friends, whilst others only come down hard if things begin to get too noisy? These and many other similar questions suggest that the classroom is a very complex environment, full of complex behaviours that may be interacting, supporting, conflicting and reinforcing each other all at the same time!

Whatever your educational experiences have been, the aim of this book is to try to give you an insight into the world of education as psychologists view it. Each chapter provides an overview of the important issues involved in that specific area, and an account of some relevant theory and research. In addition, some applications of that theory and/or research to improve the educational experience of students will be considered.

The chapters are organised in line with the topic and sub-topic areas contained in the OCR A2 specification and so each consists of three main sections that mirror the specification. Each chapter is self-contained, but occasional cross-references have been made where it was thought desirable to do so. This has, however, been kept to a minimum in order for the chapters to be used in the way that best suits you.

Wherever possible, the information, especially that of a statistical nature, is as up-to-date as possible, something which would have been more difficult without the advent of the internet. You, of course, can seek out even more up-to-date research, statistical and other evidence, by visiting the websites listed at the end of each chapter. They are not a comprehensive guide to internet resources on education, but should give you a starting point for further investigation of the topics covered in this book should you wish to extend your studies further.

Assessing educational performance

one

Introduction

The last thing that will happen to you as an A level psychology student is that you will be assessed. Why? I'm sure you've asked yourself this on many occasions, especially on the eve of an exam!

According to the DES Task Group on Assessment and Testing, 'promoting...learning is a principal aim of schools. Assessment lies at the heart of this process. It can provide a framework in which educational objectives may be set, and pupils' progress charted and expressed. It can yield a basis for planning the next educational steps in response to [learners'] needs. By facilitating dialogue between teachers, it can enhance professional skills and help the school as a whole to strengthen learning across the curriculum and throughout its age range' (Nicholls, 1999, p.116).

This quotation should tell you that assessment is not a form of torture devised by sadistic teachers with nothing better to do, but is, in fact, an integral part of the educational process and is central to effective teaching and learning.

Assessment of learning by teachers or examiners is not the only type of assessment that occurs in the educational system however. Some students are, for a variety of educational or behavioural reasons, referred to educational psychologists who assess them using a range of psychometric tests such as personality inventories, IQ tests, self-esteem questionnaires and so on.

This chapter therefore will consider the following areas:

- types and limitations of psychometric tests
- types of performance assessments at different ages
- implications of assessment and categorisation.

Types and limitations of psychometric tests

Psychometric tests may be defined as 'instruments of "mental measurement" and include personality scales along with measures of mental ability such as intelligence, creative thinking, linguistic ability and so on' (Coolican, 1996, p.84). They are primarily used in the education system for the identification of those students who may require additional support in learning, either because they show exceptional ability in one or more areas (what is usually referred to as giftedness), or because they possess some form of learning difficulty such as dyslexia. They may also be used to diagnose problem behaviours and, to assist schools that practice it, in selection or streaming of students into ability groups.

There is a wide variety of psychometric tests, far too many to be detailed in a book of this size, so the intention here is to consider just enough to give you a grounding in the principles and uses of psychometrics in education. For that reason, we will focus on intelligence tests, but you should bear in mind that the underlying principles of validity, reliability and standardisation apply to all psychometric testing.

MEASURING INTELLIGENCE AND INTELLIGENCE TESTS

The first intelligence test was devised by Alfred Binet and Theodore Simon who, in 1905, were commissioned 'by the Parisian education authorities to devise methods of identifying those children who were too "feeble-minded" for education in normal schools' (Fontana, 1995, p.97). These methods basically consisted of a series of verbal and practical problem-solving exercises that older children found easier than younger ones and 'brighter' children found easier than 'less bright' children. In addition, Binet and Simon decided that the scores on the tests should be standardised to allow comparison of any individual child with the norm for their age and thus allow calculation of a child's mental age. Thus, children aged six scoring the same as most six-year-olds on these tests would have a mental age of six, but if a six-year-old child scored the same as most eight-year-olds, then her mental age would be eight.

Terman, an American psychologist, developed the concept of mental age and gave us the formula for the calculation of a person's intelligence quotient or IQ. This formula is $MA/CA \times 100 = IQ$, where MA is mental age and CA is chronological age. Thus a child with a mental age and a chronological age of 6 would have an IQ score of 100 (MA (6)/CA (6) $\times$ 100 = 100). What would the IQ score of a child with a chronological age of 8 and a mental age of 10 be? I hope you arrived at the same answer as me, an IQ of 125.

This straightforward way of measuring IQ, however, assumes that MA increases in line with CA for the majority of the population. MA as measured by the Binet-Simon test (and others like it) seems to stop developing in the late teenage years and thus an average 36-year-old would probably score the same as most 18-year-olds. The resultant calculation would yield an IQ score of 50. This is obviously wrong, and so today, 'the calculation of IQ has become more sophisticated. It is now based on *norm referencing*' (Banyard and Grayson, 1996, p.171). An individual's IQ is now expressed in terms of how many standard deviations it is away from the mean, with the mean being scaled to the convenient score of 100. Alternatively, it may be stated as a standard age score that indicates the percentage of similar aged people who scored higher and lower on the test.

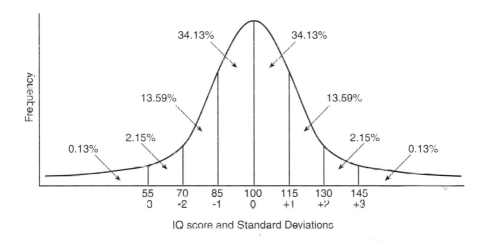

IQ score and Standard Deviations

• **Figure 1.1:** The Normal Distribution Curve, showing IQ score, standard deviations above and below the mean and percentage of the population achieving particular scores

Underlying the approach to IQ measurement is the idea of the normal distribution. Crudely put, the normal distribution implies that there are very few very intelligent people and very few very unintelligent people in the general population, with the vast majority lying somewhere in between these two extremes. If we accept this notion, and most intelligence tests are constructed as if this was the case, then we can construct a distribution curve to show the spread of different IQ scores throughout the population. Figure 1.1 above shows the normal distribution curve for an IQ test with a standard deviation of 10. This curve can be used to identify what percentage of the population lie above or below any IQ score.

Knowing what percentage of the population is likely to have very high or very low IQ scores is obviously useful for those involved with education at a policy level. At its simplest, they have an estimate of how many children are likely to need additional support at either end of the 'intelligence continuum' and so can plan accordingly.

As for what intelligence tests are actually like, Table 1.1 provides some examples from two of the most commonly used tests, the Stanford-Binet test which is used for measuring IQ in children and the Wechsler Adult Intelligence Scale, Revised Version (WAIS-R), which, as the name suggests is used with adults (aged 16–74 years).

• **Table 1.1:** Some items from the Stanford-Binet (1973) and two of the scales of the WAIS-R (adapted from Gross, 1996)

Stanford-Binet	WAIS-R
Children of three should be able to: Point to objects that serve various functions (e.g. 'hat – goes on your head') Repeat a list of two words or digits (e.g. 'cat' and 'dog', 'four' and 'six')	Verbal Scale (none of these sub-tests is timed) 1. Information – assesses general knowledge 2. Comprehension – ability to use knowledge in practical settings (e.g. 'What is the advantage of keeping money in a bank?')
Children of four should be able to: Discriminate visual forms (e.g. squares, circles and triangles) Define words (e.g. 'ball' and 'bat') Repeat ten-word sentences, count up to four objects, solve problems (e.g. 'By daytime it is light, at night it is ...)	3. Arithmetic – assesses ability to solve 'mental' arithmetic 4. Similarities – abstract thinking (e.g. 'In what ways are a book and TV alike?') 5. Digit span – attention and Short Term Memory (STM) (e.g. repeating a string of digits in the same/reverse order)
Children of nine should be able to: Solve verbal problems (e.g. 'tell me a number that rhymes with sticks') Solve simple arithmetical problems (e.g. selecting a die with six spots because the number of spots are the same as that shown on a two-spot and a four-spot die added together) Repeat four digits in forward and reverse order	6. Vocabulary – knowledge of word meaning Performance Scale (all sub-tests are timed) 1. Picture completion – assessment of visual alertness and memory by spotting missing items in drawings 2. Picture arrangement – assessment of sequential and social understanding by arranging a series of pictures to tell a story
Children of twelve should be able to: Define words (e.g. 'skill' and 'muzzle') Repeat five digits in forward and reverse order Solve verbal absurdities, e.g. 'One day we saw several icebergs that had been completely melted by the warmth of the Gulf Stream'. What is foolish about that?	3. Block design – ability to perceive and analyse patterns by copying pictures using multicoloured blocks 4. Object assembly – jigsaws used to test ability with part–whole relationships 5. Digit symbol – ability to memorise and order abstract visual patterns

The WAIS was developed in 1939 by David Wechsler because he felt the Stanford-Binet was not appropriate for adults and also that it was overly reliant on language skills. It was one of the first tests to measure separate abilities or aspects of intelligence (Atkinson, Atkinson, Smith and Bem, 1993). A similar test for children, the Wechsler Intelligence Scale for Children (WISC), has also been developed.

This point about assessing different aspects of intelligence raises a fundamental question about the nature of intelligence. Is it a single entity, is it a multi-faceted entity, or is it a hypothetical construct that is useful for understanding and predicting peoples' behaviour? This is one of the most hotly contested debates that psychology has seen, and it is far from being resolved.

Very basically, the debate centres around whether or not intelligence is an actual entity that can be objectively measured in the same way as a physical characteristic, as was argued by Spearman, Terman and Burt, or whether it is more appropriate to think of it as a descriptor for behaviour as psychologists, such as Heim and Estes consider it to be (Hayes, 1994).

There is not space here to delve deeply into this debate, but, as Hayes (1994) points out, reification of intelligence (defining it as a concrete object) has political implications. If intelligence is an actual entity then different people can possess different amounts of it and therefore it is easier to argue that the amount people have is fixed. This very quickly leads us down the road of Eugenics, the philosophy that argues that, for the good of society, those with less intelligence should be discouraged or even prevented from breeding. Thus, one implication of using intelligence tests to label children as 'feeble-minded' is that their human right to bear children is in danger from those who subscribe to the eugenicist philosophy. This may seem far-fetched, but history tells us that many states in the USA passed laws that resulted in the compulsory sterilisation of those learning-disabled young people who lived in state-run institutions. Similar reports have recently surfaced about Sweden, and not so long ago a local authority in the UK entered into a court case to compulsorily sterilise a young woman with Down's Syndrome on the basis that she lacked the intellectual capacity to make a decision about whether or not she was capable of raising a child.

(Reliability, Validity and Standardisation)

The theme link box in Chapter 3 on learning and teaching styles contains an overview of the issues of reliability and validity of measurement scales and the principles outlined there apply equally to psychometric testing, and assessment in general. In this theme link, we shall look at the issue of predictive validity a little more closely and also consider the importance of standardisation for psychometric tests.

If an assessment score is closely correlated with future performance, then that assessment is said to have predictive validity. This means that we can use the assessment to predict the likelihood of future academic success or failure. The big question for us is, 'Do IQ tests have predictive validity?' This is an important question since, if they do not, then their use as selection and streaming instruments should be abandoned. Atkinson, Atkinson, Smith and Bem (1993, p.466) state that 'youngsters who achieve higher scores on tests like the Stanford-Binet and Wechsler Intelligence Scales get better grades, enjoy school more, stay in school longer and in later life tend to have greater job success'. They also point out, however, that the degree of correlation between IQ score and academic achievement declines as students move up the academic ladder from primary school to university. Thus we could conclude that IQ tests have more predictive validity for younger students than for older ones.

Standardisation is the process of establishing a set of norms for a psychometric test for a particular population against which any individual member of that population may be compared. This is achieved by administering the test on a large sample of the population it is to be used on, and eliminating any test items that are either too easy (everyone gets them right) or too difficult (everyone gets them wrong) and ending up only with the items that *discriminate* between the testees. Ideally, the performance of the testees should conform to a normal distribution.

The implication of using an unstandardised test is that the scores generated from it become unreliable. For example, both the Stanford-Binet and the Wechsler scales were standardised only on white Americans, but have been extensively used to test the IQ of black children as well. Consequently, many black children score low on these tests, not because of a lack of intellect, but simply because the tests are culturally skewed. Stephen Jay Gould's fascinating book The *Mismeasure of Man* (1981) provides further examples of the limitations of psychometric tests including a scathing attack on the IQ testing of American soldiers conducted by Yerkes in 1916.

Types and limitations of psychometric tests
In this section we have seen that:

- there are a range of different psychometric tests that may be used in an educational context
- they are generally used for diagnostic purposes
- intelligence testing has been carried out using intelligence tests since 1905
- intelligence is thought to be normally distributed
- intelligence tests have been developed for different populations, such as children and adults
- defining intelligence is problematic
- all psychometric tests should be standardised, valid and reliable if data gathered using them is to be considered trustworthy.

Types of performance assessments at different ages

Teachers need to know whether or not they are doing their job! Possibly the most common way of checking this is to assess the learning of the students they have been teaching. The quote in the introduction to this chapter from the Task Group on Assessment and Testing indicates the central role that assessment has to play if the education of students is to have a purpose. Teachers and examiners need, therefore, to assess students at various points during their academic lives in order to be able to assist the student towards effective learning and the achievement of educational goals. These goals may of course be set by a variety of interested parties such as the teacher, the school, the Local Education Authority, the Government and, of course, the learners themselves. Before we consider the types of assessment that learners face at different ages, we need to understand something about the underlying nuances of assessment.

Types of assessment

Ideally, students should be assessed for prior knowledge and understanding at the outset of a learning programme (**initial or baseline assessment**), for developing knowledge and understanding during the course itself (**formative assessment**) and for the level of attainment of knowledge and understanding they have reached at the end of the course (**summative assessment**). In addition, both initial and formative assessment may be done for **diagnostic** purposes, to find out what a student can/cannot do and why they cannot do it, to identify misunderstandings and learning difficulties.

There are also two main categories of assessment: students can be assessed against a predetermined set of learning objectives (**criterion-referenced assessment**) or by comparison of their level of attainment with that of other students undertaking the same assessment tasks (**norm-referenced assessment**) (Baumann, Bloomfield and Roughton, 1997). Baumann *et al.* (1997, p.126) suggest, 'most tasks are assessed by a combination of these two methods. Instrumental music exams and driving tests are examples of assessment that are largely criterion-referenced. GCSE and A levels [and the new AS levels] are examples of assessment with a major norm-referencing component.'

ASSESSMENT AT DIFFERENT AGES

The National Curriculum was introduced into schools in England and Wales in 1988 as part of the Education Reform Act (ERA) and, following a number of revisions, most notably those of the Dearing Report (1994) and the Education Act (1997), we have arrived at today's situation.

• **Table 1.2:** The National Curriculum: Key Stages, Ages, School Year, Subjects and Assessments (Based on Baumann, Bloomfield and Roughton, 1997)

Key Stage	Age range	School year	Core subjects	Foundation subjects	Assessment
1	4/5–7	Reception, 1 & 2		History Geography Art Music Technology P.E. plus Welsh in schools in Wales	Baseline assessment within 7 weeks of entry into school (in schools in England) SATs levels 1–3 at end of Key Stage 1
2	7–11	3, 4, 5 & 6			SATs levels 2–5 at end of Key Stage 2
3	11–14	7, 8 & 9	English Maths Science	As Key Stages 1 & 2 plus a Modern Foreign Language plus compulsory R.E.	SATs levels 3–8 at end of Key Stage 3 (Plus 'Exceptional Performance' level for those achieving above level 8)
4	14–16	10 & 11		As Key Stage 3, but the following subjects are optional: History Geography Art Music	GCSEs graded A* to G

Table 1.2 summarises the Key Stages, age ranges, the subjects taught and the associated assessment schedule. From this table we can see that students are assessed via an initial Baseline Assessment at age 4/5 on entry to school (in England), at the end of each Key Stage via Standard Attainment Tests (SATs) at ages 7, 11, and 14, and via GCSEs at age 16.

Following on from the Dearing Report (1994), **level description/ descriptors (LDs)** were introduced to provide teachers with guidance on the level of knowledge, understanding and skills that students would need to show for attainment of each level. Teachers then use these LDs to produce a ' "best-fit" of their pupils' work to these level descriptions; in other words they will select the level description that most closely fits the work of each pupil' (Baumann et al , 1997, p.141). Pupils will therefore be assessed as 'working towards', 'working at' or 'working above' the level that matches the Key Stage they are in.

Nicholls (1999) argues that the assessment of the National Curriculum in relation to whether or not they are norm-referenced or criterion-referenced produces a confusing picture. She states:

the national criteria for assessment are encapsulated in the attainment targets as described in the level descriptors within the National Curriculum framework. The intention is that it should be a criterion-referenced system in which pupils' attainments are assessed in terms of national levels which are determined with reference to statements of attainment (Nicholls, 1999, pp.118–119).

• **Table 1.3:** The purposes of assessment (adapted from Nicholls, 1999)

• Record-keeping
• Supporting pupils in their own learning
• Providing feedback
• Measuring what pupils know, understand and can do
• Screening
• Providing information to parents, teachers, headteachers, school governors, Local Education Authorities and Central Government
• Motivating pupils
• Diagnosing learning difficulties
• Measuring standards
• Informing future planning
• Informing teachers on their own effectiveness
• Deciding on pupil grades and levels of attainment.

Assessment throughout the National Curriculum is a combination of informal (observational and question and answer sessions) and formal (tests and exams); internal (teacher-set and marked) and external (examiner-set and marked); continuous (such as coursework or GNVQ/AVCE portfolio-building) and terminal (end of course exams and GNVQ/AVCE End Tests).

Despite this variety, all of these assessments share the same purposes, which Nicholls (1999) summarises as shown in Table 1.3. Nicholls argues that, whilst all these purposes of assessment are important and should be appropriately taken into account when devising assessments, 'there are three fundamental reasons for assessment: feedback, progress [monitoring] and motivation' (1999, p.119), since these three provide the foundations for successful learning outcomes.

Section summary   **Performance assessments at different ages**
In this section we have seen that:

- assessment may be carried out at different points of a student's academic career: initial or baseline assessment at the outset, formative assessment during the course and summative assessment at the end
- assessment can be either criterion-referenced or norm-referenced
- at different ages children are assessed against level descriptors for each relevant key stage
- students are described as 'working towards', 'working at', or 'working above' the level(s) that are appropriate to the key stage they are in
- assessment has a number of different purposes, including measuring performance, screening, motivating students, supporting students in their learning and diagnosing learning difficulties
- from the above, it should be clear that assessment is much more than a teacher deciding whether or not a student has given a right or wrong answer, does or does not know something, and so on.

Implications of assessment and categorisation

Whilst the examples of compulsory sterilisation mentioned earlier are somewhat extreme, they serve to make the point that labelling someone on the basis of psychological tests can have serious repercussions. Within the education system, however, it is unlikely that the implications of labelling resulting from assessment are as dramatic as the above; nevertheless, it can have serious negative impacts on a student's academic and life-chances.

One important area to consider here is that of the **self-fulfilling prophecy** or **expectancy effect**, the situation in which a person 'comes to be' the label that is given to them. This was perfectly demonstrated in a study conducted in

1966 by Rosenthal and Jacobson (cited in Banyard and Grayson, 1996) concerned with the effects of teachers' expectations on their pupil's IQ scores. In this study, all students in all 18 classes of a US elementary school took a non-verbal IQ test that their teachers had been told would identify those children that would develop intellectually at a faster rate than their classmates. The test, of course, did no such thing, but the researchers randomly labelled 20 per cent of each class as 'bloomers' and identified the 'bloomers' to the teachers. Despite there being no significant difference between their IQ scores at the start of the academic year, the 'bloomers' showed a far greater improvement than the 'non-bloomers' by the end of the academic year.

Rosenthal and Jacobson argued that this difference in IQ scores was a result of the pupils behaving in line with the teachers' expectations of them. The teachers' expectations had, of course, been created by the labelling of some of the pupils as 'bloomers' and, by implication, others as 'non-bloomers'. Whilst there have been some criticisms of this study – for example the IQ test used (Flanagan's Test of General Ability, (TOGA)) was not standardised for use with the lower age range who showed the most improvement – support from research by Seavers on the academic achievement of siblings taught at different times by the same teachers, suggests that the self-fulfilling prophecy is a real phenomenon (Banyard and Grayson, 1996). These same authors point out that, 'if labelling someone actually causes them to behave and develop in accordance with their label, then we need as a society to be very careful about the labels that are given to people' (Banyard and Grayson, 1996, p.410).

It might be worth noting here that the labelling of students as able or less able can occur both formally, via the feedback given by teachers on students' work, and informally, via comments in class such as 'stupid boy' when reprimanding someone's inappropriate behaviour. Thus teachers need to be constantly on their guard in relation to this matter and should, ideally, strive to ascribe only positive labels to their students. As we have seen, the self-fulfilling prophesy can have both positive and negative outcomes, depending on the nature of the labelling that takes place.

Implications of assessment and categorisation

Section summary

In the final section of this chapter we have seen that:

- people are often categorised or labelled on the basis of an assessment
- these labels create expectations about people's abilities, characteristics and educational performance
- according to the self-fulfilling prophecy, people learn to behave in line with the label applied to them and the expectations that go with that label.

KEY TERMS

initial assessment
baseline assessment
diagnostic assessment
formative assessment
summative assessment
criterion-referenced assessment
norm-referenced assessment
psychometric testing
reliability
validity
standardisation
level descriptors
self-fulfilling prophecy
expectancy effect

EXERCISES

- Borrow a *test your own IQ* book from your local library (there are quite a few of these available) and take one of the tests. Is your performance comparable with your average GCSE score? What does this tell you about the validity of the IQ test?
- Ask your fellow students how tall they are. Count up the number of students in each of the following height ranges: less than 140cms, 140–149cms, 150–159cms, 160-169cms, 170–179cms, 180cms and taller. Plot the results on a graph. Is it a normal distribution?
- Look back at your old school reports, if you still have them, that is! What terms were used to describe your academic attainment? Were there any level descriptors used? If so, what do you understand them to mean about your academic ability?
- Have a discussion with your fellow students about the effects of labelling.

1   (a)   Describe some types of performance assessment at
          different ages.
    (b)   Discuss the purposes of assessment.

2   (a)   Describe types of psychometric tests used in education.
    (b)   Evaluate the use of psychometric tests in education.
    (c)   Giving reasons for your answer, suggest how psychometric
          tests could be made less biased.

Further reading

Gould, S. J. (1981) *The Mismeasure of Man*. Harmondsworth: Penguin.
A fascinating, compelling account of the misuse of psychometric testing.

Coolican, H. (1994) *Introduction to Research Methods and Statistics in
    Psychology* (2nd ed). London: Hodder & Stoughton.
Very useful for the more technical aspects of psychometric testing such as
    reliability, validity and standardisation.

Websites

http://www.queendom.com
On-line psychometric tests for you to try for yourself.

http://www.nfer-nelson.co.uk/html/edu/ahead.htm
A downloadable booklet (in pdf, so adobe acrobat needed) on current and
    future trends in educational assessment.

two

Individual differences in educational performance

Introduction

Individual differences is the area of psychology, which, like it says in the advertisement, "Does exactly what it says on the tin!" It is concerned with examining and explaining differences between individuals. Both **nomothetic** (establishing general principles which apply to all) and, to a lesser extent, **idiographic** (focusing on our uniqueness) approaches may be used in this area. Whilst much of the area of individual differences is concerned with factors such as personality and intelligence, there are two main foci in relation to educational performance – cultural differences and gender differences.

This chapter will therefore consider the following areas:

- gender and cultural differences in educational performance
- explanations for differential educational performance
- strategies for improving educational performance.

Gender and cultural differences in educational performance

GENDER DIFFERENCES

The headline on the front page of the Times Educational Supplement of May 25th 2001 (issue No. 4430) was 'Is it a boy thing? Heads say tests are unfair to girls.' This headline indicates how topical the debate around gender differences in educational performance is. The accompanying article by Julie Henry points out that in 2000, 86 per cent of girls achieved the expected level of reading at Key Stage 2 compared to 80 per cent of boys, but the expectation for 2001 was that this gap would close, if not disappear altogether, due to the nature of the material used to assess reading ability in this year's SATs.

This material used to assess reading ability was a non-fiction text about saving whales set up like a magazine and was seen as favouring boys because 'research by booksellers and a survey of more than 2,000 primary children by the Hornchurch Curriculum Centre has shown that boys prefer magazines, comics and non-fiction to the stories and novels beloved of girls' (Henry, TES, 2001).

The same article also points out that in 1999, there was an 11 per cent increase in the number of boys reaching the expected level for their age, whilst for girls, the increase was only 3 per cent. Girls did, however, still outperform boys. This difference was again put down to the nature of the material used, in this case a text about spiders which was illustrated with cartoons.

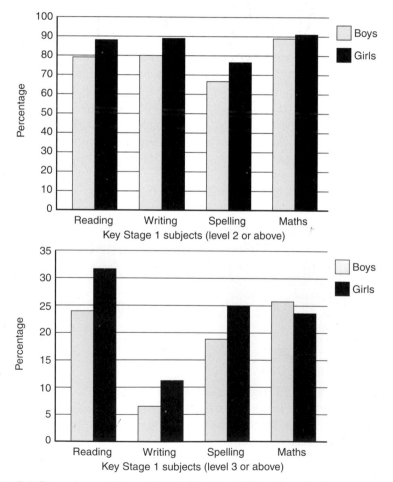

• **Figure 2.1:** Percentages of boys/girls attaining level 2/3 or above in the 2000 SATs (Adapted from DfEE standards website, 2001)

Thus, the gender differences in reading ability at Key Stage 2 seem to be related to the nature of the material that is used to assess that ability. The existence of gender differences is borne out by the statistics on educational attainment contained on the Department for Education and Employment's website, but the situation is not as straightforward as it may first appear.

Figure 2.1 above shows the percentages of boys and girls attaining level 2 or above and level 3 or above in the 2000 Key Stage 1 SATs in reading, writing, spelling and Maths. It reveals that, with the exception of Maths at level 3, girls consistently outperform boys, and this situation has remained constant for the past six years. Broadly similar results occurred at Key Stage 2. By Key Stage 3 the gap between boys and girls in English had increased to 17 per cent, but in Maths and Science the gender gap was more or less non-existent and 'this picture has remained relatively unchanged for several years' (DfEE, 2000).

The gender differences in performance at GCSE / GNVQ are summarised in Table 2.1 below, which shows that the trends established in primary and the early years of secondary school continue to the end of the GCSE examinations.

• **Table 2.1:** Recent trends in the GCSE/GNVQ National Summary Results for Boys and Girls in England (adapted from DfEE, 2000)

Year	Percentage of 15-year-old pupils:									
	Achieving 5+ A* – C GCSE's or GNVQ equivalent		Achieving 5+ A* – G GCSE's or GNVQ equivalent		Achieving 1+ A* – G GCSE's or GNVQ equivalent		Achieving no passes		Average GCSE / GNVQ points score	
	Boys	Girls	Boys	Girls	Boys	Girls	Boys	Girls	Boys	Girls
2000	43.8	54.4	86.9	90.8	93.4	95.3	6.5	4.7	36.1	41.5
1999	42.8	53.4	86.5	90.6	93.0	95.0	7.0	5.0	35.5	40.9
1998	41.3	51.5	85.5	89.7	92.3	94.6	7.7	5.4	34.5	39.7
1997	40.5	50.0	84.4	88.6	91.2	93.5	8.8	6.5	33.5	38.4
1996	39.9	49.4	84.0	88.3	91.1	93.4	8.9	6.6	33.1	37.9

From Table 2.1 we can see that girls consistently outperform boys and, in terms of the percentages achieving five or more passes at A* – C GCSEs or GNVQ equivalents, the gender gap increased by 1.1 per cent between 1996 and 2000, despite an overall improvement in performance. Thus, at GCSE level we could conclude that boys are improving, but not by as much as girls are. Moreover, the advantage that boys showed in Maths at Key Stage 1 had disappeared by GCSE, with girls sitting the 2000 examination achieving a 47 per cent A* – C pass rate as opposed to a 46 per cent rate for boys (DfEE, 2000).

The gender differences at A level are generally quite small, and tend to be more mixed, with boys in 2000 achieving more grades A – B in French but fewer in Physics for example (DfEE, 2000). In terms of Advanced GNVQs, the percentage of girls achieving a distinction is between 5 per cent and 21 per cent higher than that for boys, the latter figure being for Engineering, a subject in which the number of male candidates is about ten times greater than that of females (DfEE, 2000).

We can conclude that 'blanket statements about girls performing better than boys or vice versa are difficult to justify [and] reference should be made to particular groups of young people, to specific aspects of the curriculum or to different levels of performance' (Ruddock and Gray, 2000, p.2)

CULTURAL DIFFERENCES

Before looking at research in this area, it is worth making the point that the terms 'cultural' and 'ethnic' are often used interchangeably. There is a difference between them, however. Ethnic refers exclusively to matters related to race, whilst culture has a much wider application, and can encompass such things as class, gender and so on, as well as race. Thus, it is quite feasible for two people to share the same culture (e.g. both working class) yet come from different ethnic backgrounds (English and Welsh for example). A great deal of the research in this area has centred on ethnic differences in educational performance and this is what will be considered here.

Ethnic-related differences in educational performance have been the focus of debate since the 1960s. Several influential policy and investigative studies, including the Rampton Committee (1981), the Swann Committee (1985) and Drew and Gray (1990), appear 'to show considerable under-achievement of Caribbean and other black pupils, when compared with the average levels of achievement of white and Asian children' (Demie, 2001, p.92).

As with the gender differences already discussed, however, things are not as straightforward as they first appear. In an analysis of the performance of schoolchildren at Key Stages 1 and 2 and GCSE in the London borough of Lambeth, Demie (2001) has shown that the pattern of ethnic-related differences is quite complex and varies according to which cohort of children are being considered. Table 2.2 shows the results of Demie's study and an inspection of the figures reveals the following specific trends:

• **Table 2.2:** Performance at Key Stages 1 and 2 and GCSE, by ethnic background in Lambeth in 1988 (adapted from Demie, 2001)

Ethnic background and percentage achieving level 2 or above at Key Stage 1	Ethnic background and percentage achieving level 4 or above at Key Stage 2	Ethnic background and percentage achieving A* – C grades at GCSE
Chinese (85.7)	Chinese (77.3)	Greek (78.2)
Indian (83.0)	Pakistani (66.7)	Indian (58.6)
African (81.1)	Indian (66.0)	Irish (57.8)
English/Scottish/Welsh (79.7)	Greek (61.3)	Chinese (50.5)
Caribbean (79.8)	English/Scottish/Welsh (60.0)	Vietnamese (48.6)
Greek (78.8)	Irish ⎤ 59.3	Other white (42.7)
Vietnamese (76.7)	Vietnamese ⎦	English/Scottish/Welsh (40.3)
LEA AVERAGE (76.6)	Turkish (55.0)	Pakistani (39.0)
Pakistani (76.5)		
Other black (75.1)	Other black (54.7)	African (37.2)
Bangladeshi (72.5)	**LEA AVERAGE (53.6)**	**LEA AVERAGE (37.2)**
	African (48.3)	Bangladeshi (37.0)
Other white (67.4)	Caribbean (47.0)	Other black (33.4)
Turkish (64.7)	Bangladeshi ⎤ 46.0	Caribbean (25.6)
Irish (62.7)	Other white ⎦	Turkish (15.3)

- children from a Chinese background performed better at Key Stages 1 and 2 than those from any other ethnic group, were outperformed by children from Greek, Indian and Irish backgrounds at GCSE, but still achieved higher than the majority of other ethnic groups.
- the performance of English/Scottish/Welsh and Caribbean children declines as they get older, with the decline in the performance of the Caribbean children being far more serious, whereas that of children from Irish and Greek backgrounds improves.
- children from an African background are far more successful at Key Stage 1 than they are later on in their academic career.

Whilst it is difficult to draw firm conclusions from a single case study such as this, Demie points out that these results replicate 'findings from other studies, that Chinese and Indian pupils tend to be the highest-performing ethnic group (Thomas *et al.*, 1995; Kendall *et al.*, 1995, 1998)' (Demie, 2001, p.98). The same author also highlights the support received from other research for the relative change in positions of Bangladeshi and Caribbean pupils between Key Stage 2 and GCSE. From this study, you can plainly see that differences in academic performance do exist between ethnic groups, but it is not as simple as Asians, followed by whites, followed by blacks.

Before we look at possible explanations for differences in educational performance, it is worth noting that Demie (2001) also considered gender differences within the different ethnic groups. He found very similar differences to those reported in the first part of this chapter, i.e. girls generally do better than boys at all ages, but not necessarily in all subjects. Table 2.3 contains a summary of Demie's findings in this area.

• **Table 2.3:** Performance by Key Stage, gender and ethnic background (percentages) (adapted from Demie, 2001)

Ethnic background	% KS1 level 2 or above		% KS2 level 4 or above		% GCSE A* – C grades	
	Girls	Boys	Girls	Boys	Girls	Boys
African	84.0	78.5	50.0	46.0	41.8	27.9
Bangladeshi	75.0	70.8	43.0	49.0	41.7	32.5
Caribbean	80.7	78.5	48.0	46.0	28.6	18.3
Chinese	80.5	92.6	78.0	77.0	58.3	35.7
English/Scottish/ Welsh	79.6	75.9	63.0	59.0	40.2	40.5
Indian	84.5	80.0	63.0	67.0	58.5	58.7
Irish	13.3	83.3	66.0	56.0	40.2	47.5
Vietnamese	88.9	58.3	74.0	43.0	67.3	10.0
Portuguese	51.5	40.8	N/A	N/A	33.3	26.1
All pupils	79.4	74.4	56.0	53.0	41.2	34.6

Thus it would seem that gender differences in educational performance are cross-cultural in their occurrence. Demie's findings are supported by Ewing's (2001) summary of research conducted in the USA by Richard Coley of the Educational Testing Service. Coley found that 'in educational attainment, females across all racial/ethnic groups have made dramatic progress, pulling even with –

and in some cases, surpassing – males. White, black and Hispanic females are more likely than their male counterparts to graduate from college' (Ewing, 2001, p.2). You may also want to consider the possibility that boys and girls have different learning styles, and information on this can be found in Chapter 5.

Gender and cultural differences in educational performance

Section summary

In this section we have seen that:

- girls outperform boys in reading, writing and spelling in Key Stages 1 and 2
- boys outperform girls in Maths in Key Stages 1 and 2
- for the past 5 years at least, girls on average outperform boys at GCSE, including Maths
- differences at A level are small, and not necessarily related to traditional sex-stereotyped subjects, e.g. girls do better at Physics and boys at French
- girls also outperform boys at Advanced GNVQ, even in male-dominated subjects such as Engineering
- there are variations within these general trends: to simply claim that girls are academically outperforming boys across the board is to misrepresent the facts
- in general terms, irrespective of age, children from a Chinese or Indian background tend to outperform children from most other ethnic backgrounds
- again, in general terms, irrespective of age, children from Caribbean, Bangladeshi and Turkish backgrounds tend to be outperformed by children from most other ethnic backgrounds
- for children from some ethnic backgrounds, e.g. Greek, Irish, Pakistani, their relative educational performance compared with children from other ethnic background varies with age
- there is evidence that gender differences, similar to those reported in the previous section, run across all cultural groups
- blanket statements about the educational performance of individual ethnic groups should be treated with caution.

Explanations for differential educational performance

We have already seen that the likelihood of an individual student attaining a high level of educational success is related to both their gender and their ethnic background. Explanations for the differences in performance described above come from two areas, biological explanations and socio-psychological explanations.

BIOLOGICAL EXPLANATIONS

The basic argument here is that differences in behaviour, including that of educational performance, are the result of differences in biology. Although there are undoubtedly **biological differences** between males and females, to suggest that difference in educational performance is biologically determined is to also suggest that the male and female brain are different. Is there any evidence to support this?

Gross (1996) cites a study by Dorner (1968) in which a small part of the 'sex-centre' of a rat's brain was destroyed. Following this lesion, the male rat behaved as if it were female. As Gross points out, however, generalising from rats to humans is very difficult. The same author also reports that research reveals a greater degree of hemispheric specialisation in men than in women. 'For example, when performing spatial tasks, a man's right hemisphere seems to be more active while with women both hemispheres are activated. In fact, the right hemisphere is generally the dominant one in men and the left in women, which could explain why men are generally superior at spatial and mathematical tasks and women at verbal tasks' (Gross, 1996, p.584).

On the face of it, this could explain girls outperforming boys in English. As we have seen, however, girls also achieve a much higher 'pass with distinction' rate in Engineering (a subject that requires both mathematical and spatial skills) than boys, and this seems to contradict the claim that sex-differences in performance are biologically determined.

Interestingly, Boyle (1998) investigated the relationship between menstrual cycle moods and symptoms and attainment across the whole of the Australian curriculum and found a large number of small but significant negative relationships. This would suggest that girls, who experience these menstrual cycle moods and symptoms, should perform at a lower level than boys who obviously do not experience them. Yet we have seen that in the vast majority of subject areas, girls consistently outperform boys. Indeed, we could, if we felt inclined, suggest that the gap would be even greater if girls' menstrual cycle moods and symptoms did not have a negative impact on their studies.

The fact that gender differences in educational performance occur across cultures and change over time and in relation to specific subjects, suggests that the biological explanation is weak. Whilst it could be argued that these cross-cultural gender differences would seem to support the biological approach, historically, the picture has not always been what it is today, and cultural forces are far more important in shaping educational experiences, expectations and performance, than biology.

Applying the biological explanation to cultural differences is even more problematic. All human beings, no matter what their ethnicity, have far more in common with each other biologically than they have differences. Indeed, there is a far greater variation of genetic differences *within* ethnic groups than *between* them. This point is most convincingly put by Stephen Jay Gould who states:

....*Homo Sapiens* is tens of thousands, or at most a few hundred thousand, years old, and all modern human races probably split from a common ancestral stock only tens of thousands of years ago. A few outstanding traits of external appearance lead to our subjective judgement of important differences. But biologists have recently affirmed – as long suspected – that the overall genetic differences among human races are astonishingly small. Although frequencies for different states of gene differ among races, we have found no 'race genes' – that is, states fixed in certain races and absent from all others (Gould, 1981, quoted in Gross, 1996, p.738).

Thus, it would seem that biological explanations for cultural differences in educational performance are also very weak.

Theme link – Gender and cultural differences in educational performance and ethnocentrism

'Ethnocentrism' is the term used to describe the process of judging other groups of people according to the norms and standards of behaviour that apply to the group to which you belong. When we assess educational performance and find that different groups of students, such as boys/girls, Indian/Chinese/English/Caribbean and so on, perform at different levels, there is a high risk of interpreting those differences in an ethnocentric way. For example, if we describe those groups as being more, or less, academically able or intelligent than the group to which we belong, then we are effectively judging them *against our standards*. This is particularly true if the assessment used is based on our cultural heritage and perspective. You may be aware of Gould's (1982) criticisms of Yerkes' use of IQ tests with American soldiers in 1915, which is a prime example of ethnocentrism in relation to race/ethnicity and intelligence.

As discussed in this chapter, there may be reasons other than ethnicity and gender, such as social class or cultural bias in assessments (the male bias apparently shown in the 2001 SATs reading tests mentioned earlier, for example). Therefore, we must guard against making judgements of different groups' relative educational performance unless we are aware of all the factors that impact on that performance.

The consequences of ethnocentrism in gender and cultural differences in educational performance can, at the least, result in prejudice and discrimination. At its worst it lends support to eugenicists (people who argue that, for the benefit of society, those of lower intellectual ability should be prevented from having children) and lays the ground for another holocaust. These consequences strengthen the point that differences in performance must be interpreted with caution.

SOCIAL-PSYCHOLOGICAL EXPLANATIONS

Research in this area suggests a range of social-psychological factors that can account, at least partially, and to a far greater extent than the biological approach, for gender and cultural differences in educational performance. These factors include poverty/socio-economic class and attitudes/beliefs and expectations. These factors are now explored.

poverty/socio-economic class

According to Powney (1997, p.4), 'Although Sammons *et al.* (1983) identified seven factors which can be used to predict the statistically increased risk of low attainment at age 11, poverty is the most obvious key feature and one which has a clear impact on reading and maths attainment across not only gender but also ethnic groups.' Pupils from socio-economically deprived areas are more likely to suffer ill-health, higher levels of absenteeism, more likely to attend poorly resourced schools, and receive less support at home than pupils from higher up the socio-economic scale (Powney, 1997). Powney's claims for the importance of poverty are backed up by both Demie (2001) and Shuttleworth (1997), who found a positive correlation between socio-economic class, as measured by eligibility for free school meals, and GCSE scores in pupils in Northern Ireland.

attitudes/beliefs and expectations

Beloff (1992, p.309) states, 'Stereotypes say women are not as clever as men, they are hare-brained (which is hard on hares), they can only think about concrete things, they have butterfly minds, they are illogical'. Such beliefs could explain the differences in attainment in Maths and English shown by boys and girls earlier in this chapter: it could be that children are socialised into gender identities and gender roles that deem it acceptable for girls to possess high levels of linguistic skills and boys to be more rational and logical.

That this might be the case is borne out by the evidence. As we have seen, girls are now beginning to outperform boys in what, traditionally, have been considered masculine subjects: Maths, Physics and Engineering. This coincides with a societal change in beliefs about gender roles and a gradual decline in the sex-stereotyping of school subjects (Archer and MacDonald, 1996), at least as far as girls are concerned. Rudduck and Gray (2000) state that girls are now more likely to take 'masculine' subjects, but the reverse is seldom seen.

As a consequence, girls' expectations of what they can achieve, and the expectations of their parents and teachers, are probably higher today that they were even just ten years ago, whilst that of boys has remained more or less static. As you will have seen in the study on teacher's expectations by Rosenthal and Jacobson (1996) detailed in Chapter 1, expectations can be a powerful influence on performance.

Linked to this is the notion of the **self-fulfilling prophecy**. This is where a person comes to behave in line with the labels given to them as a result of the expectations that they and others have of them. Thus, girls perform well at English because they are expected to by others and, equally importantly, because, as a result of socialisation, part of their self-image depends on being good at English. Thus they conform to the label of 'being good at English'. Boys, on the other hand, self-fulfil the prophecy of not being skilled at languages, but being more mathematically inclined. This explanation is not only able to account for the historical differences between genders, but also for the current situation in which girls are outperforming boys in what were traditionally considered male subjects. As already stated, society's attitudes are changing, and with that change comes changes in expectations, and therefore changes in the relative educational performance of boys and girls.

Expectations also have an impact on cultural differences in educational performance and Fuller (1980, cited in Powney, 1997) found that black girls from deprived socio-economic backgrounds in London had higher aspirations than their male counterparts and consequently distanced themselves from their peers because they did not want to be held back by them. 'Eight years later, Eggleston (1988) reported that schools had avoided putting African-Caribbean pupils into academic or exam streams in case they were "disruptive" or "unrealistically ambitious"' (Powney, 1997, p.5).

This statement is a damning indictment of the attitudes, beliefs and low expectations that have built up about the academic ability of black children, and is supported by research conducted by Rubovits and Maehr in 1988. In this study, white trainee teachers were informed that the classes they were about to take as part of their teaching practice were of mixed ability. Individual students were identified to the trainee teachers as being 'gifted' or 'non-gifted'. This categorisation was, in fact, done randomly, and bore no relationship to the child's actual ability. Each class, therefore, was seen as containing four groups of students: white 'gifted', white 'non-gifted', black 'gifted' and black 'non-gifted'. During the course of the year, the trainee teachers' interactions with the students were observed. The results showed that the labels given to the students influenced the amount and type of interaction with the trainees. For example, in terms of positive interaction, the white 'gifted' students received most, followed by white 'non-gifted', black 'non-gifted' and finally black 'gifted'. In terms of negative interaction, this order was reversed.

Rubovits and Maehr suggest that the poor treatment given to those black students labelled 'gifted' can be explained by these students not matching the trainees' stereotypes of black students, and so the label, 'gifted', was ignored. The authors also suggest that trainee teachers need to be made aware of their prejudices and stereotypes so that they are in a position to develop and utilise strategies to counter them, a point that leads us onto the final section of this chapter.

Section summary **Explanations for differential educational performance**
In this section we have seen that:

- there is evidence from animal studies that supports the idea of male and female brains being different
- there is evidence that men have greater hemispherical specialisation than women, especially for spatial and mathematical tasks
- this is contradicted by the evidence that 21 per cent more girls than boys achieve distinction in Advanced GNVQ engineering, for example
- ethnic groups are more genetically similar than they are different
- biological explanations for differential educational performance are generally weak
- social-psychological explanations, however, are better supported by the evidence of examination statistics
- there is a positive relationship between socio-economic class and educational performance
- people's attitudes and beliefs about education are related to educational performance
- students perform in line with their own and others' expectations, including teachers'.

Strategies for improving educational performance

Few would disagree that the education system should attempt to ensure that every child that passes through it should be given the opportunity to realise their potential. As we have seen, however, factors such as social class, societal expectations, stereotypes and prejudice, often work against this. So what can be done to mediate this situation and offer a more balanced academic experience for all students, irrespective of gender or ethnicity? Rudduck and Gray (2000) and Sukhnandan, Lee and Kelleher (2000) suggest a number of strategies that can be used to address this situation. Among these are:

- single-sex groupings
- role modelling
- mentoring
- additional learning support.

single-sex grouping

The use of **single-sex groupings** in co-educational schools developed out of research that showed that, in a mixed environment, boys tended to dominate the classroom interactions and also that there was a definite gender preference for certain subjects (Rudduck and Gray, 2000). By teaching the genders separately, their competence, confidence in and liking for 'non-traditional' subjects can be improved. Although initially introduced to deal with the disadvantages faced by girls in areas like Maths and Science, single-sex groupings are now being used to support boys in improving their performance in subjects such as English.

In addition, single-sex groups provide a means of developing an understanding of the social construction of gender roles, and the opportunity to develop the confidence to change, if that is what they want. Rudduck and Gray (2000) point out, however, that it is too early to assess the effectiveness of this strategy, because changes in academic performance tend to be relatively slow in occurring.

role modelling

Role modelling strategies are based on the behaviourist principles of social learning theory. Simply put, this theory states that behaviour is learned as a result of observation followed by imitation of the behaviour of others. Those who are observed and imitated are known as role models. Schools can use role modelling in two ways.

Firstly, they can bring guest speakers into the school, such as female engineers and plumbers, male nurses and so on, who have successfully challenged stereotypes, in order to give students the opportunity to see that change is possible. The Government's call in the last few years for more men to apply for training as primary school teachers and for more fathers to volunteer to lead reading sessions in their children's primary schools, can be seen in this context. Secondly, they can ensure that traditional stereotyping within the school itself is avoided, for example, by ensuring that their senior management team reflects the cultural and gender balance of the society in which we live.

mentoring

Lefrancois (1994, p. 399) defines a **mentor** as an 'individual engaged in a one-to-one teaching/learning relationship in which the teacher (mentor) serves as a fundamentally important model with respect to values, beliefs, philosophies and attitudes, as well as a source of more specific information'. Thus, many schools are utilising the services of former students who have succeeded academically to engage with current pupils, as a way of providing those children with additional support from a role model they can relate to. Although initially introduced with pupils in years 10 and 11, this practice is now being utilised across the whole range of secondary schooling and even, in some cases, in primary schools (Rudduck and Gray, 2000).

additional learning support

In the not too distant past, students who were thought to be underachieving would have been sent for remedial education. This was seen as an indication that the child was not academically able and the reason for that lay within the child. To put it bluntly, they were considered 'thick as pig muck'! Thankfully, today, we have realised that the need for **additional learning support** should be a right of every student, because the reasons for their underachievement are usually related to broader factors beyond their control, such as those described earlier in this chapter. Additional learning support is a way of supporting a student in developing a range of skills and techniques to assist them in overcoming any difficulties they may face in their learning. It may involve one to one tuition, the development of study skills, the provision of specialist equipment and so on.

Sukhnandan, Lee and Kelleher (2000) and Demie (2001) both strongly emphasise the point that one of the major factors affecting the performance of some ethnic minority children in their early school career is that their command of English, as a result of it not being used as the primary language at home, is not that advanced. Table 2.4 shows the relationship between fluency in English and attainment at Key Stage 2, and clearly demonstrates that improved fluency is reflected in improved achievement.

• **Table 2.4:** Key Stage 2 performance and stages of English language fluency, by ethnic group (adapted from Demie, 2001)

Stages of English fluency	Percentage of students obtaining Level 4 or higher at Key Stage 2		
	African	Bangladeshi	Portuguese
Bilingual stage 1	18	0	0
Bilingual stage 2	26	22	30
Bilingual stage 3	58	51	73
Bilingual stage 4	80	93	85

Thus, schools should develop policies of assessing each individual student's additional learning support needs and integrate the provision of these into the mainstream curriculum. The first step towards achieving this is to regard the need for additional learning support as a *right* from the outset of the child's school career, rather than something brought in to remediate the situation when the child underachieves. After all, prevention is better than cure!

Strategies for improving educational performance

In this final section we have seen that:

- a number of strategies can be used to improve educational performance and to work against the effects of gender and cultural factors
- single-sex grouping can be used to overcome male dominance in the classroom
- single-sex grouping can be used to overcome sex-stereotyping of academic subjects
- it is too early to say how effective this strategy is
- role modelling can be used within the classroom through the use of guest speakers
- educational institutions should attempt to ensure that their senior management team reflects the gender and cultural diversity of the catchment areas that they serve
- mentoring is an effective way of building students' expectations by pairing them on a one to one basis with a former, successful, student from similar background.

KEY TERMS

educational performance
idiographic
nomothetic
SATs
biological
self-fulfilling prophecy
single-sex grouping
role modelling
mentoring
additional learning support

EXERCISES

- The average IQ is 100. What do you estimate yours to be? Compare your estimate of your IQ with other people's estimates of their IQ. My prediction is that boys will give higher estimates than girls? Why is this?
- Discuss the pros and cons of working in single-sex groups – you may want to try this in single-sex groups and then compare answers!

1   (a) Describe some gender and cultural differences in educational performance.
     (b) Discuss possible causes for these differences in educational performance.

2   (a) Outline gender differences in educational performance.
     (b) Compare and contrast biological and socio-psychological explanations for these differences.

3   (a) Describe some cultural differences in education.
     (b) Evaluate cultural differences in education.
     (c) Giving reasons for your answer, suggest some strategies that could be used to overcome cultural differences in education.

Further reading

Gipps, C. & Murphy, R. (1994) *A Fair Test? Assessment, Achievement and Equity*. Open University Press.
A comprehensive account of this area.

Demie, F. (2001) Ethnic and gender differences in educational achievement and implications for school improvement strategies. *Educational Research*, *43*, 1, 91–106 (also available at http://www.tandf.co.uk/journals).
The introduction to this report of a case study into ethnic and gender differences in an LEA gives a very good overview of this area.

Websites

http://www.standards.dfee.gov.co.uk/genderandachievement/
The official government website for all things educational. This page has statistics and reports relating to gender and education.

http://www.scre.ac.uk/spotlight/spotlight64.html
The website of the Scottish Council for Research in Education.

http://www.ncrel.org
The website of the North Central Regional Educational Laboratory, an American not-for-profit organisation. Contains lots of useful information, albeit with an American slant.

http://www.nfer.ac.uk/summary/genderclass.htm
The website of the National Foundation for Educational Research, a gem of a site for British-based educational research.

three 3

Special educational needs

Introduction

The purpose of this chapter is to provide an overview of the issues of special educational needs (SEN) and giftedness. It will briefly consider how these features are defined and assessed and the educational strategies that can be used to assist children identified as having special educational needs or being gifted. To the layperson, the term special educational needs usually means children who have some form of handicap, or disability; giftedness, on the other hand, is usually considered as indicating a particular ability or talent. It may seem somewhat perverse, therefore, to consider what appear to be polar opposites in the same chapter.

However this is not the case, for as we shall see, it has long been recognised that gifted students, like learning disabled students, have special educational needs which must be met if they are to derive full benefit from their educational careers. In addition, there are some students who are gifted *and* learning disabled (Maker and Udall, 1985; Baum, 1990), and this paradox will also be considered in this chapter.

This chapter will therefore focus on the following areas:

- definitions, types and assessment of special educational needs (including gifted children)
- causes and effects of specific learning difficulties or disabilities
- strategies for educating children with special needs.

Definitions, types and assessment of special educational needs

DEFINING SPECIAL EDUCATIONAL NEEDS

According to the Department for Education and Employment, a child is considered to have **special educational needs**:

> if he or she has a learning difficulty which needs special teaching. A **learning difficulty** means that the child has significantly greater difficulty in learning than most children of the same age. Or, it means a child has a disability that needs different educational facilities from those that schools generally provide for children of the same age in the area. The children who need special education are not only those with obvious learning difficulties, such as those who are physically disabled, deaf or blind. They include those whose learning difficulties are less apparent, such as slow learners and emotionally vulnerable children. It is estimated that up to 20 per cent of school children may need special educational help at some time in their school career (DfEE, 1994, p.1).

This definition of a student with special educational needs is the statutory definition which schools in England, Wales and Northern Ireland currently have to work with, but it was not always so.

> Historically, special education has operated on what might variously be described as a 'handicapped', 'medical' or diagnostic' model. Whatever the term used, the common feature was the use of a 'within child' explanation of special educational needs. Children within these models are seen as *possessing* a handicap, a learning difficulty, 'ESN(m)ness', emotional disturbance etc. (Dessent, 1987, p.5).

This approach assumes that there is a sharp divide between those students in need of special education and those who are not. The publication of the Warnock Report by the Department of Education and Science (the forerunner of today's DfEE) in 1978 saw a sea change in the way special educational needs were thought about. Warnock conceived of special educational needs as being a continuum of need for assistance with education, rather than a continuum of ability or disability. This meant that at one end of the continuum there would be a relatively large number of children in need of a certain level of assistance to support their learning, whilst at the other end there would be relatively few who required far more extensive support. This continuum of special educational needs is shown in Figure 3.1.

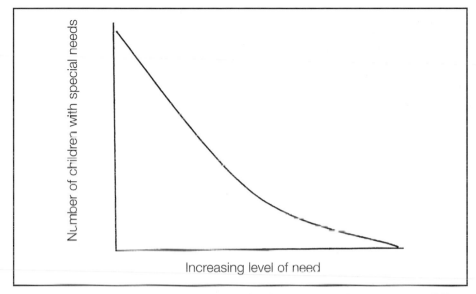

Increasing level of need

• **Figure 3.1:** The continuum of special educational needs (adapted from Dessent, 1987)

Thus, the Warnock report saw a shift in thinking about special educational needs away from one centred on what was 'wrong' with the child to one which focused on what was needed to provide the child with the best possible opportunity in the education system. This is still the case today, and the change in thinking reflected in the Warnock report has since been reflected in the 1996 Education Act (Part IV) and its associated Code of Practice (currently undergoing a comprehensive review) which local education authorities have to consider when drawing up policies for children with special educational needs (CaF, 2000).

Before going on to look at some individual learning difficulties that result in special needs, it is important to consider how, irrespective of the cause and type of learning difficulties, they are assessed within the education system.

ASSESSING SPECIAL EDUCATIONAL NEEDS

The 1996 Education Act (Part IV) and its associated Code of Practice, which replaced the 1993 Education Act, laid down a clearly defined assessment process with regard to special educational needs.

• **Table 3.1:** The five stages of special educational needs assessment (based on CaF, 2000)

Stage of SEN assessment	Parties involved in the assessment	Action to be taken
Stage 1	School (through teacher and Special Educational Needs Co-ordinator (**SENCO**)	Teacher records concerns about child's learning difficulties and discusses them with parent(s) and SENCO
Stage 2	Teacher, SENCO, Parent(s)	SENCO assesses child's learning difficulties and, together with the teacher, reviews the additional support offered in the classroom to the child. SENCO also consults parent(s) and draws up an Individual Education Plan (IEP) for the child.
Stage 3	Teacher, SENCO, Parent(s), Outside expertise (e.g. Educational Psychologist), Headteacher	If child's special educational needs are not met by provision arranged under stage 2, then additional advice from outside agencies, such as the Educational Psychology Service, or specialist teachers will be sought. If child's progress is not as expected, the headteacher will decide whether or not to ask the local education authority to make a statutory assessment.
Stage 4	Local Education Authority (LEA), School, Education Adviser, Doctor, Educational Psychologist, Health Visitor/Therapist Parent(s)	The LEA considers the need for an assessment and, if appropriate makes one. They will ask for and consider reports from a variety of individuals and agencies that have had involvement with the child or are in a position to offer some insight into the child's learning difficulties. If appropriate a statement of special educational needs is issued.
Stage 5	LEA, School, Parent(s)	If a statement is issued, then the LEA and school have to take immediate steps to make the provision for the child's special educational needs set out in it.

It stressed that the statutory assessment should be undertaken with the full involvement of the parent(s) who have a significant contribution to make to the assessment. There are five stages to the formal assessment of special educational needs and these are detailed in Table 3.1. It can be seen from this table that the assessment of the child becomes more formal and more in-depth as the stages are passed through, and this reflects the increasing severity of the learning difficulty a child may have.

The **statement of special educational needs**, which is the legally recognised document of the special needs of an individual, should contain six major items that are aimed at ensuring the child's needs are met. These are shown in Table 3.2.

• **Table 3.2:** The major items of a statement of special educational needs (adapted from CaF, 2000)

• All the provision to be provided by the school/LEA
• The number of hours additional support, including specialist help
• Any special equipment the child requires
• Any diagnosis which indicates special provision – e.g. speech therapy
• Educational targets for the child, reviewed annually
• Any modification to the National Curriculum.

Thus the **assessment of special educational needs** is a multi-modal, multi-agency assessment. It involves the parents drawing up a profile of the child – focusing on such things as the child's health, play activities, relationships, behaviour and so on – as well as considering more general things like comparison with other children of a similar age.

Solity and Raybould (1988) suggest that teachers adopt an *assessment-through-teaching* approach to defining a student's special educational needs. This involves the teacher drawing up an overall plan of learning outcomes for the student and the teaching methods they will use to help the student achieve those outcomes. The student's progress is monitored continuously, on a daily or weekly basis. If progress is deemed to be unsatisfactory, further intervention can be implemented, in the form of changes to the teaching methods, calling in additional support after consultation with the SENCO and parents, or even progressing further down the route towards statementing.

In addition, via the input of an educational psychologist, the assessment may well involve the administration of a variety of psychometric tests such as personality inventories, IQ tests, and self-esteem inventories, as well as assessments for specific disorders such as dyslexia, dyscalculia, dyspraxia, sensory impairments, Attention Deficit Disorder, autism and so on. Assessment may also be carried out to identify whether or not a child is gifted, and it is to this that we now turn.

GIFTEDNESS

Towards the beginning of this chapter, mention was made of the continuum of special needs. If we take that idea of a continuum and apply it to ability in its broadest sense, then giftedness is seen by many as lying towards the opposite end of this continuum to learning difficulties. But how do we define giftedness?

Marland states that 'gifted and talented children are those identified by professionally qualified persons who by virtue of outstanding abilities are capable of high performance' (1972, quoted in ERIC EC digest # E476, p.1). The idea that giftedness is identifiable and measurable by professionals is backed up by Lefrancois (1997) who states that the most common way of defining giftedness is in terms of IQ scores, with anyone scoring between 130 and 140 described as borderline gifted, whilst those scoring above 140 are labelled gifted.

Sternberg and Wagner (1982, cited in ERIC EC digest # E476) however, suggest that giftedness is characterised by insight skills that allow a person to separate relevant from irrelevant material, combine isolated pieces of information into a coherent whole and relate newly acquired information to that already in their possession. The person who has these skills would then be able to manage their life in a constructive and purposeful way. It could be argued that this definition focuses on the qualities or characteristics of the gifted person and the behaviour they display, as opposed to the statistical definition implied by Marland.

Renzulli's definition of giftedness (1986, cited in Lefrancois, 1977) can be seen as occupying the middle ground between the two approaches discussed above. He argues that giftedness is shown by those who display: above average general or specific ability (which may be evidenced from achievement and/or an IQ score); high levels of task commitment (or persistence and motivation); high levels of creativity (which may be seen in the generation of novel ideas and/or problem solving).

Despite the problems of definition outlined above, there is general agreement that gifted people share a range of characteristics, but, as with all aspects of human nature, there exist individual differences in the degree and number of these characteristics which any one gifted individual may possess. Table 3.3 summarises these characteristics.

• **Table 3.3:** Some general characteristics of gifted children (adapted from ERIC EC digest # E476)

- Shows superior reasoning powers and marked ability to handle ideas.
- Shows persistent intellectual curiosity; asks searching questions.
- Has a wide range of interests, often of an intellectual kind; develops one or more interest to considerable depth.
- Is markedly superior in quality and quantity of written and/or spoken vocabulary.
- Reads avidly, and absorbs books well beyond his/her age.
- Learns quickly and easily and retains what is learned.

- Shows insight into mathematical problems and grasps mathematical concepts readily.
- Shows creative ability or imaginative expression in such things as music, art, dance, and drama; shows sensitivity and finesse in rhythm, movement and bodily control (what Gardner (1983) calls bodily-kinaesthetic intelligence).
- Sustains concentration for lengthy periods and takes responsibility for academic work.
- Sets realistically high standards for self and is self-critical in evaluating achievement.
- Shows initiative and originality in academic work; shows flexibility of thought.
- Observes keenly and is responsive to new ideas.
- Shows social poise and an ability to communicate with adults in a mature way.
- Gets excitement and pleasure from intellectual challenge; shows an alert and subtle sense of humour.

GIFTED BUT LEARNING DISABLED

Baum (1990, p.1) asks, 'How can a child learn and not learn at the same time? Why do some students apply little or no effort to school tasks while they commit considerable time and effort to demanding creative activities outside of school?' She answers this question by suggesting that these are typical behaviours of students who are both gifted and have learning difficulties at one and the same time. Baum uses the term **gifted but learning disabled** to identify such children. She also points out that, because giftedness and learning difficulties are seen as lying at opposite ends of the same continuum, many professionals fail to acknowledge the possibility of giftedness and learning difficulties being displayed by the same student. The existence of these two characteristics is often a feature of Asperger's Syndrome, one of the disorders that comprises Autistic Spectrum Disorder, and this contributes to the delay in diagnosis of this disorder that frequently occurs. This approach may also lead to educators, parents and psychologists paying more attention to the giftedness whilst not identifying, or even ignoring, the learning difficulty or vice versa.

Maker and Udall (1985) suggest that assessment of a gifted but learning disabled student should include individually administered IQ tests, diagnostic achievement tests, creativity assessments, parental interviews, observation of peer interactions, perceptual tests, visual–motor co-ordination tests and a range of other forms of assessment. On the basis of the information gathered, decisions can be made by a committee familiar with the student (teacher, headteacher, educational psychologist, parent) as to whether the student displays both giftedness and learning difficulties and the precise nature and degree of each.

Section summary   **Definitions, types and assessment of special educational needs**

In this section we have seen that:

- there is a statutory definition of special educational needs
- historically, SEN was considered a 'within child' concept
- the Warnock Report (1978) put forward the idea of a continuum of special educational needs, with the focus on learning rather than disability
- assessment of special educational needs is a legal requirement and must be conducted in line with a code of practice
- assessment has a multi-modal, multi-agency approach
- there are five stages to assessment: each successive stage reflects an increased severity of learning difficulty
- the outcome of assessment may be the production of a Statement of SEN
- initial assessment should be an assessment-through-teaching
- assessment may involve the use of psychometric tests, administered by an educational psychologist
- giftedness can be defined by IQ score
- gifted children share certain characteristics
- gifted children may also have a learning disability.

Causes and effects of specific learning difficulties or disabilities

THEORIES OF CAUSATION

There are numerous theories about the causes of learning difficulties and, according to Selikowitz (1998), most are based on the premise that there is some impairment of brain functioning. He points out that these theories however, 'are not mutually exclusive, since each may explain one step in the chain of events that gives rise to specific learning difficulties' (Selikowitz, 1988, p.32). This position is summed up in Figure 3.2.

In Figure 3.2 we can see that Selikowitz is proposing that either genetic factors, or environmental factors, or an interaction between environmental and genetic factors, results in some form of brain damage and/or malformation and/or dysfunction and/or maturational lag, which in turn leads to a cognitive or information processing deficit. It is the nature of this deficit that leads to the

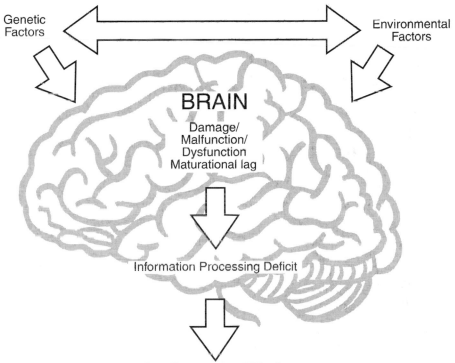

Genetic Factors

Environmental Factors

BRAIN

Damage/
Malfunction/
Dysfunction
Maturational lag

Information Processing Deficit

Specific Learning Difficulty

• **Figure 3.2:** Causal factors that may lead to a specific learning difficulty (adapted from Selikowitz, 1998)

diagnosing or labelling of the specific learning difficulty. Thus, at least in general terms, the causes of specific learning difficulties can be thought of as *bioenvironmental* in nature.

SOME SPECIFIC LEARNING DIFFICULTIES

dyslexia

Dyslexia can be defined as difficulty in learning the symbols involved in a written language and comes in several forms, of which the most common are auditory dyslexia (dysphonetic dyslexia), visual dyslexia (dyseidetic dyslexia) and mixed or classic dyslexia (dysphonetic and dyseidetic dyslexia). It is a chronic neurological disorder that interferes with the ability to recognise and process written symbols. It tends to run in families and is three times more prevalent in boys than girls. Dyslexia is estimated to affect approximately 3–5 per cent of the population (SNER, 2001). Students with dyslexia may experience learning difficulties in the academic areas listed in Table 3.4 below.

∘ **Table 3.4:** Learning difficulties related to dyslexia (adapted from SENR)

> - Spoken language: delays, disorders, or discrepancies in listening and speaking
> - Written language: difficulties with reading, writing and/or spelling
> - Arithmetic: difficulties in performing arithmetical functions or in comprehending basic concepts
> - Organisational skills: difficulty in organising her/himself and/or her/his work
> - Thinking skills: difficulty in organising and integrating thoughts and planning ahead.

dyscalculia

This is the mathematical equivalent of dyslexia, and can be defined as difficulty in learning, understanding and using the symbols involved in mathematics. The student with **dyscalculia** may also have spatial difficulties such as a difficulty in lining up numbers in columns.

autistic spectrum disorder

Autistic spectrum disorder is the term given to a 'family of biologically based disorders which comprise a number of different medically diagnosed conditions' (Jordan and Jones, 1999, p.2), as shown in Table 3.5.

∘ **Table 3.5:** The diagnostic categories of autistic spectrum disorder contained within ICD-10 and DSM-IV (based on Jordan and Jones (1999)

> - Autism
> - Autistic disorder
> - Atypical autism
> - Rett's syndrome
> - Childhood degenerative disorder
> - Asperger's syndrome
> - Pervasive developmental disorder
> - Pervasive developmental disorder, not otherwise specified
> - Semantic pragmatic disorder

The classification of autistic spectrum disorders given in Table 3.5 is an amalgamation of the two major classification systems used by psychiatrists and clinical psychologists to diagnose mental disorders. ICD-10 is the World Health Organisation's *International Classification of Diseases, 10th revision,* published in 1992, Chapter 5 of which is concerned with *Mental and Behavioural Disorders,* whilst DSM-IV refers to the American Psychiatric Association's *Diagnostic and Statistical Manual of Mental Disorders, Fourth Edition,* published in 1994 (Gross, 1996). There is not space here to consider the full range of autistic spectrum disorders and so only a brief account of autism itself will be attempted.

Kanner in 1943 defined autism as an 'inability to relate ... in the ordinary way to people and situations ... an *extreme autistic aloneness* that, whenever possible, disregards, ignores, shuts out anything that comes to the child from outside' (cited in Rosenhan and Seligman, 1989, p.549).

Autism is characterised by the features set out in Table 3.6, and has a prevalence of 2–4 children in every 10,000, similar to the incidence of deafness in children and twice the levels of blindness. Boys with autism

• **Table 3.6:** The main characteristics of autism

Main characteristic	Example of behaviour
Restricted language development	Echolalia: repetition of phrases, words or sounds. Whilst part of normal language development in babies, in children with autism it persists throughout childhood.
Insistence on sameness	Autistic children develop a preference for things and events to occur in the same way again and again. They can become extremely upset if their routine way of doing things is interrupted.
Restricted social development	Baron-Cohen argues that many autistic children lack a *theory of mind*. That is, they fail to recognise that other people can hold thoughts and beliefs about the world that are different to their own. This results in a lowered ability to interact on a social level, since a large part of that interaction involves interpreting what others think and believe.
Inconsistent intellectual development	Generally poor on verbal tests of intelligence, but may score well above average on spatial tasks and tasks involving rote memory. Some autistic children, so-called *autistic savants*, show 'islands of intelligence', that is, they show giftedness in one particular area such as ability to use numbers, art and music.

outnumber girls by 4:1 (Baron-Cohen, 2001). Psychodynamic psychologists like Bruno Bettleheim (1967, cited in Rosenhan and Seligman, 1989) have proposed that autism results from the child actively withdrawing from the insensitive, aloof, physically and emotionally distanced response of its parents, especially the mother.

There is little evidence to support this view, since not all autistic children experience such 'emotional refrigerator' parenting, and not all children of such parents are autistic. In fact, Cantwell, Baker and Rutter (1978, cited in Rosenhan and Seligman, 1989) point out that autistic children experience the same range of parenting styles as do non-autistic children. Similarly, behaviourist claims that autism is a result of the child modelling their parent's behaviour can also be largely discounted on similar grounds.

The most prevalent current ideas as to the causes of autism suggest that it is a neurological disorder, possibly resulting from the effects of a particular peptide on the brain. You may also be familiar with the ongoing debate about the possibility of autism being related to an infant's reaction to the MMR (measles, mumps and rubella) triple vaccine. The fact that this alternative physiological cause has been suggested implies that the precise cause of autism is yet to be established. This in turn highlights one of the shortcomings of the physiological approach: our lack of knowledge of the detailed working of the body's biochemistry and how it interacts with the environment.

Section summary — **Causes and effects of specific learning difficulties or disabilities**

In this section we have seen that:

- learning difficulties may be the result of genetic/biological factors, environmental factors, or an interaction between the two which produces an informational processing deficit
- depending on the nature of this deficit, different types of learning difficulty can be identified, including dyslexia, dyscalculia and autistic spectrum disorder
- each disorder is characterised by its own unique set of characteristics
- Chapter 7 on disruptive behaviours contains details on attention deficit (hyperactivity) disorder, AD(H)D, which you may like to use as an example of a specific learning disorder.

* **Table 3.7:** Pros and cons of mainstream placement for children with autistic spectrum disorders (Jordan and Jones, 1999)

Pros	Cons
Access to 'better' models of social and linguistic behaviour.	Many staff and pupils to be understood and adjusted to.
Easier access to full curriculum resources including the National Curriculum.	Curriculum may not be designed to meet the special needs of the pupil.
Specialist subject teaching to develop child's interests and strengths.	Less likelihood of staff having knowledge of autistic spectrum disorders.
Peers available as a resource for 'buddies' and teaching aides.	Poorer staff–pupil ratio to identify and meet needs and develop skills, except when extra adult support is allocated.
Higher expectations to develop knowledge and skills and improve life chances.	Less realistic expectations and less availability of curriculum methods that reduce stress and enable learning.
Broader opportunities for curriculum development, qualifications and career choice.	Fewer opportunities to learn in functional contexts and to address difficulties that interfere with life chances.
Locational opportunity for social integration within a community and for family involvement.	Poorer understanding of isolating effects of the disorder and fewer resources to support families.
Opportunities to spread awareness and tolerance of autistic spectrum disorder in society.	Fewer opportunities for staff to share problems/experiences/successes with others and gain support.
A better context for developing understanding of, and conformity to, the cultural values and rules of society.	Assumptions of 'normality' as a framework offer less understanding and less tolerance of difference.

Strategies for educating children with special needs

STRATEGIES FOR EDUCATING CHILDREN WITH SPECIAL NEEDS USING AUTISM AND DYSLEXIA AS EXAMPLES

mainstream or specialist?

There is much debate about whether or not special educational needs should be met in special schools, mainstream schools or, as Jordan and Jones suggest in relation to autistic spectrum disorders, a combination of the two: 'It is our view that children with autism would benefit most from early specialist education within which the child can develop the skills needed to learn in less specialised settings at a later date (Jordan and Jones, 1999, p.5). They point out that there are advantages and disadvantages to educating children with autistic spectrum disorders in mainstream schools and colleges and these are reproduced in Table 3.7.

Jordan and Jones (1999) accept the fact that these pros and cons are generalisations and things may differ from one school to another. It could also be argued however that the points they make are equally as valid for other learning difficulties as they are for autistic spectrum disorders, and today the emphasis is more and more towards the *integration* of children with special needs into mainstream schools and colleges. This trend has been given additional impetus through the granting of royal assent to the Disability Rights in Education Act in March 2001. This act enshrines in law the right of any person with special educational needs to have those needs met in mainstream schools and colleges should they so wish.

STRATEGIES FOR EDUCATING CHILDREN WITH AUTISM

The key to the development of any educational strategy for children with special needs is to draw up a detailed picture of what those needs are and then to devise ways of meeting those needs. This may mean focusing on different needs at different times as well as, or instead of, attempting to take a more holistic approach to the student. Powell (2000) makes a number of proposals for the effective teaching of children with autism as a way of pointing towards the development of a pedagogy for autism. These are summarised in Table 3.8. This shows that strategies for educating children with autism must not only include specific tasks organised and carried out in particular ways, but also demand a careful and thoroughgoing reflection on their practice on behalf of the teacher.

• **Table 3.8:** Some teaching strategies for use with children with autism (based on Powell, 2000)

- Processing of concrete, visible and spatial information is better than that of abstract, invisible, temporal information for many children with autism. Teachers needs to utilise ways of presenting information visually, in ways that are more suitable for the child, e.g. teach telling the time using a digital rather than analogue clock face as the former may be easier to process than the 'invisible' areas of a typical clock face.
- There is a need to focus on the teacher–pupil relationship and for teachers to regard themselves as *learners* of how the child can be enabled to learn, and the pupils as *teachers* of how they learn.
- Some information may need to be presented in an asocial context due to the difficulties autistic children have with social situations, e.g. the use of computer-based instead of teacher based learning activities.
- The computer can be used as an interface between teacher and pupil to facilitate learning about social behaviour.
- Teachers need to provide opportunities for pupils with autism to share their experiences and understanding with others as a precursor to developing common, negotiated understanding, e.g. the student might 'teach' a stooge how to complete a jigsaw puzzle that they are very familiar with.
- Teachers need to enable those with autism to progress from self-regulation to independent thinking, e.g. organising the classroom layout so that particular areas of the room become associated with particular activities by the autistic student. This gives the student some sense of control over the environment, and therefore a feeling of power and independence.
- A multi-sensory approach should be adopted when appropriate. That is, information should be presented that stimulates *all five senses*, rather than just relying on the visual and auditory modalities. This may provide the basis for moving towards more conceptually-based education.
- The learning environment needs to be predictable and ordered if learning is to be effective. This includes the behaviour of the teacher.

STRATEGIES FOR EDUCATING STUDENTS WITH DYSLEXIA

As we have seen, children with dyslexia may experience learning difficulties in one or more specific areas, and so any strategy aimed at supporting these children educationally must take this on board. As a consequence, there have been a number of different strategies developed, with different skills being targeted by them. Table 3.9 summarises some of these strategies.

• **Table 3.9:** Some strategies for helping students with dyslexia overcome specific learning difficulties (based on Selikowitz, 1998)

Area of difficulty	Example of strategy used to target the area of difficulty
Reading errors	Carefully structured (phonetic) schemes such as the _Alpha-to-Omega_ and _Orton-Gillingham-Stillman_ methods. Both of these teach sounds first and gradually move up to words. They also emphasise the need for constant revision to compensate for possible poor retention.
Spelling errors	Phonetic errors, where the child may have difficulty with converting phonemes (sounds) to graphemes (written symbols), can be addressed by teaching the pupil to break words down into their component parts. Lexical errors, where the word 'sounds right' but 'looks wrong' (e.g. writing 'rite' for 'right') suggest that the child has problems remembering the appearance of words. This can be addressed by using tasks that practise the visual recall of familiar words.
Writing errors	These may be due, for example, to motor-planning difficulties (or dyspraxia) in which the child has difficulty in planning and carrying out organised sequences of motor movement. The child may be able to produce all of the individual movements needed to write a word, but cannot string them together in the appropriate manner. Part of the strategy to improve such a child's writing may involve firstly correcting the child's posture and the way that they hold a pen. They may then be taught manuscript writing (where letters are written individually, like the writing you are currently reading), then precursive writing (where 'tails' are added to individual letters (_such as this_), before progressing to cursive writing (_or 'joined-up' writing like this_). The degree to which they progress through these three stages is dependent on the severity of their learning difficulty.

Whilst Selikowitz, who is a consultant developmental paediatrician, does not mention it, implicit in all the above strategies is the importance of reinforcement of behaviour. In effect, these strategies are based on the behaviourist notions of behaviour shaping, as described in Chapter 4, with the student receiving both extrinsic (praise from the teacher) and intrinsic (increased feelings of self-worth) reinforcement as progress is made.

The nature–nurture debate is concerned with the issues of environmental and physiological determinism, which we examine in theme link in the chapter on motivation (Chapter 6). In relation to special educational needs, however, this debate is particularly important.

Originally, the nature–nurture debate focused on the question 'Which is responsible for behaviour, biology or environment?' It soon became apparent that this was a false question, since it is impossible to separate humans from their environment and study the effects of their biology in isolation, and vice versa, of course. So the debate shifted to examine the question 'How much of behaviour is the result of biology and how much the result of environmental factors?' Again, it became obvious that this was an inappropriate question, since it was nothing more than a subtle re-wording of the first one. Today, the question that is asked is 'In what ways do biology and environment interact?', and it is this question that is relevant to special educational needs.

Whilst many of the learning difficulties that bring about special educational needs undoubtedly have a biological basis, if we were to simply accept their physiological determination, then we would also have to accept that until we have more fully developed techniques such as genetic modification, then there is little we can do to assist individuals with such learning difficulties.

By asking the latter question, however, we immediately acknowledge that, whilst we may not be able to remove the disorder, we can make environmental changes to compensate to some degree for the difficulty in learning that the disorder brings with it. The entire development of educational strategies for people with special educational needs is based on this approach.

Thus, nature may well be the cause of the learning difficulty, but the environment can and does influence the *impact* that it has on the individual's educational experience and achievements.

STRATEGIES FOR EDUCATING GIFTED CHILDREN

As has been suggested, giftedness can be seen as another example of special educational needs and, as such, raises similar concerns as to the most effective strategies for educating such children. As early as 1937 Neville was calling for gifted children to be educated separately from the mainstream because he felt that this would allow their special educational needs to be met in a coherent way. Others argue that it is better to educate gifted children in mainstream schools because the social isolation resulting from separate provision may lead to difficulties in relating to others in later life.

Lefrancois (1997) asserts that there are two approaches to educating gifted students, **acceleration** and **enrichment**. The former consists of progressing gifted children more rapidly than non-gifted students through the educational system, even though they follow the same curriculum. This is why we find 12, 13 and 14-year-olds at university, for example. Enrichment provides gifted children with additional and different school experiences from their peers in order to allow them to fulfil their potential.

It has been argued that acceleration, like separate education, whilst catering for the intellectual development of gifted students, could have adverse effects on their social and emotional development. However enrichment, because the gifted students simply take on extra educational activities and are not separated from their peers, does not have such effects. Lefrancois (1997) cites Horowitz and O'Brien (1986) as saying that research has yet to establish which of these two is the best approach to take, and then argues that perhaps a system that is flexible enough to accommodate both acceleration and enrichment is the most desired situation.

STRATEGIES FOR EDUCATING GIFTED BUT LEARNING DISABLED CHILDREN

Maker and Udall (1985) suggest that there is no one ideal way of meeting the special educational needs of such students and instead an Individual Education Plan (IEP) is the way forward. Nevertheless they also point out that 'a program for gifted but learning disabled students may take one of several forms:

- primarily an enrichment programme with the student receiving additional help for the disability
- a self-contained program which focuses on both strengths and weaknesses
- primarily a remediation program' (Maker and Udall 1985, p.1).

Both Maker and Udall (1985) and Baum (1990) agree that it is important to focus on both the gift and the difficulty in an environment that values individual differences and supports the development of potential. Both also agree that the provision of **compensatory strategies** and skills is vital if the special educational needs of gifted students with learning difficulties are to be met. Table 3.10 outlines some of these compensatory strategies, which are techniques that can be used to try to counteract or compensate for specific learning difficulties.

• **Table 3.10:** Compensatory techniques for gifted students with learning difficulties (based on Maker and Udall, 1985, and Baum, 1990)

Area of concern	Compensatory strategy
Reading	Present information in a variety of ways e.g. videos, recorded speech, visits, interviews, pictures.
Organisation and management skills	Use advance organisers, brainstorming and webbing (spider diagrams) and provide essay plans. Use cognitive behaviour modification techniques to develop specific skills.
Productivity	Use technology such as calculators and computers to overcome specific difficulties with writing and arithmetic.
Work presentation	Allow students to present work in the way that is best suited to the individual. A video project is as good as an essay!
Short-term memory	Assist the student in the use of mnemonics and visualisation techniques.

Thus, if students with both giftedness and learning difficulties are to have their special educational needs met, it is important to carefully and thoroughly assess both their gift(s) and their learning difficulties and provide an individual educational plan (IEP) that adequately caters for both. This IEP should ensure that they have the opportunity to excel in those areas where they are gifted and the support needed to assist them in working to overcome those areas in which they experience difficulty.

As a final point, it is worth considering the idea that the development of strategies for special needs education can, and has, thrown up examples of good teaching practice which can be applied to all students, not just those they were initially developed for. In fact, we could consider the assessment of special educational needs to be an example of the individual profiling that humanistic psychologists would argue should be the starting point of education for all children. Once we understand the educational needs of the individual we are better placed to produce an educational programme that is tailored specifically to that individual.

Section summary

Strategies for educating children with special needs

In this final section we have seen that:

- there is a debate about whether children with special educational needs should be educated in special schools or integrated into mainstream schools or colleges
- the trend today is towards integration, and the Disability Rights in Education Act (2001) lends great support to this approach
- there are, however, advantages and disadvantages to integration
- there is a range of specific teaching strategies that can be used in the classroom to meet the special needs of students with learning difficulties
- it is important that the learning difficulty/special educational need is correctly and fully identified in order to ensure that the appropriate strategies are adopted.

KEY TERMS

special educational needs (SEN)
learning difficulties
assessment
statement of SEN
SENCO
dyslexia
dyscalculia
autistic spectrum disorders
giftedness
acceleration
enrichment
gifted but learning disabled
compensatory strategies

- Imagine you are a newly qualified teacher in a typical primary school. How would you set about determining whether or not any of the pupils in your class have special educational needs?
- Discuss with your classmates whether mainstream or specialist education is most suitable for children with dyslexia or autism.

SAMPLE EXAM QUESTIONS

1 (a) Describe some types of special educational needs.
   (b) Discuss possible causes and effects of those special educational needs.

2 (a) Outline possible causes and effects of one special educational need.
   (b) Consider strategies that could be used for improving the educational performance of a student with that special educational need.

3 (a) Describe some types and causes of special educational needs.
   (b) Evaluate these types and causes of special educational needs.
   (c) Giving reasons for your answer, suggest some strategies that could be used to meet the special educational needs of school students.

Further reading

Rosenhan, D. L. & Seligman, M. E. P. (1989) *Abnormal Psychology* (2nd ed). New York, London: Norton.
Provides a good, accessible account of specific learning difficulties.

Jordan, R. & Jones, G. (1999) *Meeting the Needs of Children with Autistic Spectrum Disorders*. London: David Fulton Publishers.
A good introduction to Autistic Spectrum Disorders, with some thought-provoking case studies.

Selikowitz, M. (1998) *Dyslexia and Other Learning Difficulties: The Facts* (2nd ed). Oxford: Oxford University Press.
A straightforward approach to dyslexia.

Websites

http://www.dfee.gov.uk/sen/
The special educational needs section of the Department for Education and Employment's website. Contains details on the statutory regulations relating to SEN.

http://www.geocities.com/sen_resources/
The website of the Special Educational Needs Resources organisation. Gives accessible information on those learning difficulties most likely to be encountered in mainstream education.

http://www.autisminfo.com
An American site with lots of information about autism and links to other related sites.

http://www.oneworld.org/autism_uk/index.html
The website of the National Autistic Society which gives news, articles and information on all aspects of autism.

http://www.bda-dyslexia.org.uk/
The British Dyslexia Association's website with articles, news and information. Especially good for information on how to support someone with dyslexia.

http://www.inclusive.co.uk/
A commercial site about special needs and technology. Offers free downloadable accessible media players and a good set of links to other related sites.

four

Perspectives on learning

Introduction

Any example of human behaviour can be approached from a variety of perspectives. Suppose you sign your name on a piece of paper. From a *biological* or *physiological* perspective this act can be described as the firing of various nerve cells that activate the muscles that move your fingers and arm to grasp the pen and drag it across the surface of the paper. From a *phenomenological* or *humanistic* perspective, signing your name can be seen as an expression of your self, your signature is a way of telling the world who you are.

A *behavioural* psychologist may interpret this as the appropriate response to the stimulus of having an autograph book shoved under your nose. A *social psychological* explanation may focus on the meaning of the signature. If signed on a cheque then it represents an agreement between yourself and the person you make the cheque out to. In the same way that different perspectives can be applied to the relatively simple act of signing one's name, so they can be applied to the complex world of education.

Whilst all psychological perspectives can be applied to education, probably the three most important, which this chapter will focus on, are:

- The behaviourist approach
- The cognitive approach
- The humanistic approach.

It is worth pointing out here that the following chapter on learning styles and teaching styles also contains examples of how cognitive and humanistic approaches have been applied to education.

Behaviourist applications to learning

INTRODUCTION

At the end of the 19th century, psychology was in its infancy. The main method of investigation was something called *introspection* (literally, looking inwards), and was carried out by spending a great deal of time trying to experience and give a descriptive account of what it was like to think. Then, in 1913, an American called John B. Watson argued that this was all very well, but what psychology should be was a science and, as a science, it should adopt scientific methods. This meant measuring behaviour in a laboratory since this was the only true objective scientific approach. Thus, for Watson, the only proper concern of psychology should be observable behaviour, as that is the only type of behaviour that can be objectively measured. Thus was **behaviourism** born.

There are three basic strands to behaviourism, *classical conditioning*, *operant conditioning* and *social learning theory*, and each has something to say about how behaviour is learned. For behaviourists, this means all behaviour, as they argue that we are capable of only basic biological functioning at birth and, like any other animal, our behavioural repertoire increases as a result of experience in an environment. Of most importance in education are:

- classical conditioning
- operant conditioning.

CLASSICAL CONDITIONING

basic principles

Early in the last century, a Russian physiologist called Ivan Pavlov was carrying out research into the digestive system of dogs (why? I don't know … but somebody had to do it!) which involved measuring the amount of salivation at different stages of the digestive process (see Figure 4.1). One day he noticed something unusual: a dog started to salivate at the sight of the food bucket *before* it had been fed. Pavlov, knowing that looking at buckets doesn't lead to salivation, realised that somehow or other the dog had come to associate the bucket with being fed. Therefore the sight of the bucket elicited the same response as being fed – salivation.

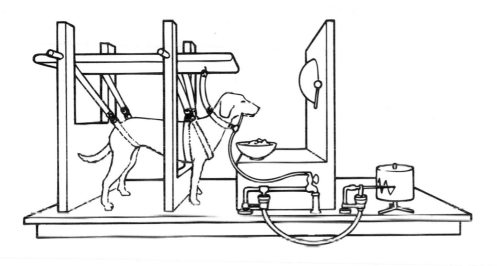

* **Figure 4.1:** The apparatus used by Pavlov in his experiments on conditioned reflexes (from Gross, 1997, p.157)

Being a scientist, Pavlov then immediately set about trying to discover whether he could get the dog to salivate over something else that does not naturally produce this behaviour. One of the things he tried was ringing a bell. Sure enough, when he rang the bell, the dog failed to salivate. He then rang the bell again, and this time fed the dog immediately after the sounding of the bell. The dog, of course, salivated. He repeated this pairing of the bell with the food a number of times and then rang the bell without feeding the dog. The dog still salivated. Pavlov had succeeded in teaching the dog to salivate to the sound of a bell!

This process of learning by association (the dog had come to associate the bell ringing with being fed and so responded to it as if it had been fed) is known as **classical conditioning**. Pavlov provided a series of technical terms that are used to summarise the process of classical conditioning and these are shown in Figure 4.2.

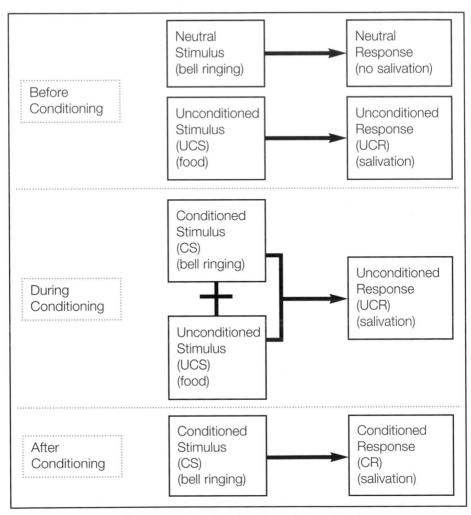

• **Figure 4.2:** A diagram showing the principles of classical conditioning

the application of classical conditioning to education

What subjects did you not enjoy when you were doing your GCSEs? Which teachers did you not like that much? Are the two related? It is possible that you came to dislike a subject because you associated it with a teacher who always shouted at you, or gave you some other reason to dislike her/him. In terms of the classical conditioning formula, the teacher's shouting is the **UCS**, the negative attitude towards the teacher is the **UCR**, the subject is the **CS** and the negative attitude towards the subject is the **CR**. If you form a dislike for a subject it is quite likely that you will not try your best to achieve in it as much as you will in subjects you like and so your academic performance in the disliked subject will be lower than it might be. In order to avoid this happening, teachers should strive to provide as many positive associations with their subject as they can.

An extreme, but very important outcome of this process of associating school with unpleasant experiences is the development of school phobia. This is more than a mere dislike of a teacher or a subject; it is a state of anxiety and fear brought on by the thought of going to school, and has obvious implications for the sufferer's education.

The principles of classical conditioning, in the form of **systematic desensitisation**, can, however, be used to alleviate this phobia. Systematic desensitisation, in a basic sense, is where the sufferer is gradually and systematically exposed in steps of increasing intensity to the phobic object. In the case of school phobia, the first step may be to get the child dressed for school, but keep them in a relaxed state at home. This would then be followed by taking them out of the house to the bus stop. When they can achieve this with no undue anxiety, catching the bus and riding past the school would be the next step. Successive small steps would then follow until the point is reached where the child willingly returns to school. It is important that the child associates each step of this process with feelings of relaxation rather than anxiety, otherwise the phobia will remain.

This is one example of the application of behaviourist principles to education. Others will be discussed after the principles of operant conditioning have been outlined.

OPERANT CONDITIONING

basic principles

As we have seen, in classical conditioning, the learned behaviour (the CR) is very similar to the natural response to the unconditioned stimulus: dogs naturally salivate to food. However, if we wanted to teach the dog something completely new (such as turning off the television) classical conditioning would be of no use. What unconditioned stimulus would the dog automatically respond to by turning off the television? To train the dog to turn off the TV, you must first get it to turn it off and afterwards reward it with food or praise. If you keep doing this, eventually the dog will learn to turn off the TV when told to.

A lot of human behaviour is like this: responses (behaviours) are learned because they operate on, or affect, the environment. This form of learning is known as **operant conditioning** and was first investigated in a series of experiments in 1898 by E. L.Thorndike, who was trying to show that there was little difference between human and non-human learning (Atkinson, Atkinson, Smith and Bem, 1993). In a typical experiment, a hungry kitten is placed in a 'puzzle box' (see Figure 4.3), a box whose door is held closed by a simple latch. A piece of fish is placed outside the box and, since the kitten is hungry, it is motivated to escape from the box to get to the fish. Initially it will simply try to reach out for the fish, but when this fails, the kitten moves around the box, trying different things until eventually it accidentally hits the latch, the door opens and the kitten is rewarded by eating the fish.

• **Figure 4.3:** A puzzle box (from Zimbardo, 1977, p.319)

Thorndike found that when he repeated this procedure, the kitten spent less and less time scrabbling about in the box until it reached the point when it would undo the latch almost immediately. It can now be said to have learnt this behaviour. This demonstrates what Thorndike termed the **law of effect,** that behaviour which has a pleasant consequence for the organism is more likely to be repeated. The cat eliminated irrelevant behaviour and repeated the latch-opening behaviour because only the latter resulted in a positive consequence (feeding on the fish).

There is more to operant conditioning than the law of effect, however, and it was B. F. Skinner who was responsible for fully establishing its principles as we understand them today. Using what has become known as a 'Skinner Box', Skinner showed that rats and pigeons could learn very complex behaviours through operating on their environment and the associated consequences of that behaviour.

In this type of experiment a rat or a pigeon would be placed into a Skinner box – a box in which there is a lever with an empty food dish underneath it (see Figure 4.4). Initially, the rat or pigeon would explore the box and at some point would press the lever. The rate at which the lever is pressed is used as a baseline for comparison. After the baseline has been established, the experimenter activates a food magazine, which delivers a single food pellet into the food dish in the box whenever the lever is pressed. Now, every time the pigeon presses the lever it is rewarded by receiving food. The pigeon very quickly associates the lever-pressing with being fed and so increases its amount of lever-pressing behaviour. The food acts as reinforcement for the lever-pressing and thus we have the principle that *behaviour which is reinforced is learned*.

• **Figure 4.4:** A pigeon in a Skinner Box

Skinner also showed, by stopping the delivery of food pellets when the lever was pressed, that learned behaviour would cease (i.e. **extinction** will take place) if no reinforcement were forthcoming.

The reinforcement of behaviour by providing some form of reward after the behaviour has been performed is known as **positive reinforcement**. There is another type, **negative reinforcement**, in which an organism performs a behaviour not to bring about a pleasant consequence, but rather to remove an unpleasant consequence of not behaving. Using a Skinner box with a metal floor attached to a low-voltage electricity generator, a rat is rewarded for pressing the lever by having the current turned off (thus avoiding an unpleasant stimulus, the continuation of the electric shock) rather than receiving a food pellet (evoking a pleasant stimulus). Both positive and negative reinforcement serve to increase the performance of a desired behaviour. **Punishment** serves to stop behaviour from happening. If the current is turned on when the rat presses the lever, then the rat very quickly stops pressing the lever.

The use of positive reinforcement can result in the learning of quite complex behaviours. In the same way that Skinner taught pigeons to play table tennis, you can teach your dog to turn off the TV (although why you should want to do this, except perhaps to annoy the rest of your family, is beyond me!). This can be achieved through the use of **behaviour shaping**. The dog is rewarded for behaviours that come closer and closer to the desired behaviour of pressing the off switch on the TV. You might start with rewarding the dog with a food treat or praise for walking towards the TV, requiring it to get increasingly closer to the off switch in order to get each reinforcer, until eventually the dog presses its nose against the switch and the TV is turned off. If you utter the command 'TV off' at the same time, you can get the dog to turn the TV off only when you tell it to. This shows another aspect of operant conditioning, **discrimination**, the ability of the organism to distinguish between the stimulus it has been conditioned to and other similar stimuli.

Whilst there is a lot more to operant conditioning than has been outlined above, the major principles that have been established now allow us to look at how they can be applied to the world of education.

the application of operant conditioning to education

The principles of operant conditioning can be applied to education in two major ways:
*   the production of programmed learning exercises
*   classroom management.

Programmed learning consists of a series of steps or frames in which students are presented with material and, if they produce the correct response, they are reinforced through appropriate feedback and can then move on to the next frame. There are two types of programmed learning, linear and branching. The former is by far the simpler, consisting of a series of questions that the student has to answer. After they answer the question the correct response is revealed (irrespective of whether the student got it right or not) and they move on to the next one, and so on until the end of the exercise (see Figure 4.5).

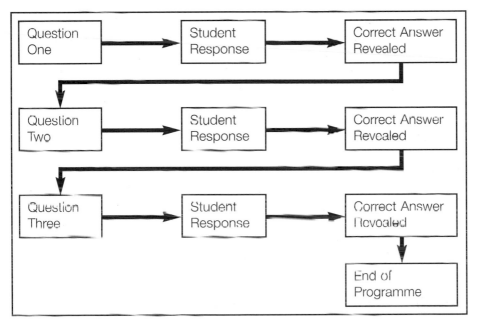

• **Figure 4.5:** A linear programme

In a branching programme, however, if a student gives an incorrect response, they are directed to additional information/questions that are designed to allow them to understand their mistake before they move on to the next item, as shown in Figure 4.6. It can be seen, therefore, that whilst linear programmes are useful tools for checking knowledge, branching programmes are able to assess understanding and result in additional learning.

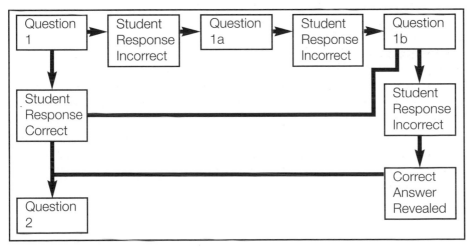

• **Figure 4.6:** A branching programme

Lefrancois argues that 'instructional programs [as he terms programmed learning] are largely of historical interest only, although some of their principles may be useful in ordinary classrooms' (1997, p.327). The useful principles include active responses from students to teachers' questions, immediate feedback to students on their responses and the resultant error-free learning that occurs. The use of this approach can be seen in some of the teaching of ICT in today's educational system, particularly in self-study units actually carried out on computers.

The use of the principles of operant conditioning, and particularly behaviour shaping, to control and manage disruptive classroom behaviour will be discussed in greater length in Chapter 7. It is enough here to point out that the basis of effective classroom management is for the teacher to positively reinforce desired or appropriate behaviour via the use of reinforcers such as praise, gold stars, 'good work' stamps (see Figure 4.7) and so on, and to negatively reinforce or punish inappropriate behaviour through the use of detention, extra homework or the threat of these punishments.

• **Figure 4.7:** The Good Work stamp that my students strive to achieve!

Section summary   **The application of behaviourism to education**
In this section of the chapter we have examined the following topics:

- the behaviourist view of human nature, with its theory that all behaviour is learned
- two theories of learning: classical conditioning and operant conditioning
- applications of these theories to education: the use of systematic desensitisation to treat school phobia (classical conditioning), an approach to teaching called programmed learning (operant conditioning) and classroom management through the use of positive and negative reinforcement and behaviour shaping (operant conditioning).

Cognitive applications to learning

INTRODUCTION

The **cognitive perspective** has been defined as 'the scientific study of mental events' (Gagne, 1985, p.4). It is concerned with how we process or encode, store and retrieve information. This also means that cognitivists are concerned with understanding how we interpret, organise and use information to understand the world around us. In relation to education, therefore, the cognitive approach stresses the importance of 'cognitive strategies and a recognition of the importance of relationships among items of information' (Lefrancois, 1994, p.156).

This means that the curriculum, and the way it is delivered, needs to be organised to allow the important relationships between pieces of information to be developed and established. These informational relationships are often referred to as **schemas** or **schemata**. In order to develop schemas and therefore understanding, learners should be deliberately encouraged to develop strategies that allow effective perception, interpretation, organisation, analysis, evaluation, storage and retrieval of information.

There are a number of different ways of applying these principles to education, but we will consider only three:

- Bruner's *discovery learning* approach
- Ausubel's *expository teaching and reception learning* approach
- Vygotsky's *zone of proximal development*.

bruner's discovery learning approach: basic principles

Bruner, like Piaget and others, subscribed to a way of thinking called **constructivism**. He argued that every individual constructs their own version of reality through their experiences, the cognitive processes that they use on these experiences and the schemas that they develop. For Bruner, the learner is an active information processor who needs to simplify and make sense of their environment through the formation of concepts or *categories*. This is achieved by the learner taking common elements from all of their relevant experiences and developing basic rules or *coding systems* about how these categories relate to each other. He therefore sees our understanding of the world as a complex associative arrangement of categories and coding systems.

The role of the school is to provide the vehicle that allows the development of categories and coding systems to occur. Central to this is the idea that that the learner is active in this process, rather than a passive receiver of information from others. In other words the learner should be educated via discovery learning.

Lefrancois defines **discovery learning** as 'the learning that takes place when students are not presented with subject matter in its final form but rather are required to organise it themselves. This requires learners to discover for themselves relationships that exist among items of information' (Lefrancois, 1994, p.158). This implies a very different role for the teacher. Their job is not to impart learning and knowledge to their students, but rather to offer guidance and support as learners discover for themselves. This inevitably means a more student-centred approach.

For discovery learning to be effective, there are a number of conditions that need to be satisfied. These are summarised in Table 4.1. According to Bruner, if a teacher is aware of these four factors, discovery learning can facilitate the transfer and retention of knowledge, increase problem-solving skills and ability and increase motivation.

• **Table 4.1:** Conditions that facilitate discovery learning

Condition	Explanation
Set	The learner is ready to discover by being prepared to look for relationships between items of information.
Need state	The learner's level of arousal should be moderate rather than too high or too low.
Diversity of training	The learner needs to be exposed to information in a range of situations in order to develop codes to organise it.
Mastery of specifics	The learner needs to be prepared to discover specific relevant information. The wider the range of information, the more likely they are to discover relationships.

the application of bruner's approach to education

As a consequence of these conditions Bruner makes a number of recommendations for the implementation of discovery learning in the classroom. Among these are:

1. The curriculum models used should facilitate the development of coding systems. Teaching should begin by providing learners with the *basic underlying principles* that give structure to the subject. For example, in the AS level OCR psychology specification, students should be made aware early on of the perspectives, themes, issues and research methods (the underlying principles) in order to allow them to develop an understanding of these principles and to be able to use them later in evaluating the core studies.

2. Any concept can be taught to a child of any age, providing that the teaching uses the **mode of representation** suitable to that age group. Children progress from sensory-motor (**enactive**) ways of thinking about or representing the world to using concrete images (**iconic**) and finally to abstract (**symbolic**) representation. So for example, in teaching the laws of chemistry, the ideal approach would be to allow the child to witness what happens when acid is poured onto metal before proceeding to a theoretical account containing formulae.

3. There should be a programmed return to topics in such a way that they are considered in increasing depth and complexity. Bruner termed this a **spiral curriculum**. This allows the learner to develop general codes relating to the information presented; the relationships between categories allows building of knowledge which is transferable and easy to recall.

4. Learners should be encouraged to make educated guesses as this can facilitate the formation of codes and therefore aids understanding.

5. Teachers should use a range of teaching aids to help in the formation of categories, as this allows learners to utilise appropriate modes of representation.

ausubel's expository teaching and reception learning approach: basic principles

Ausubel argues that discovery learning is time-consuming and not demonstrably more effective than the traditional approach, where the teacher gives the learner all the information they require in its finished form (**expository teaching**) and the learner learns that material (**reception learning**) (Ausubel and Robinson, 1969). Moreover, meaningful verbal learning, which is what Ausubel is really concerned with, generally takes place via expository teaching. By *meaningful verbal learning*, Ausubel means that an object, or concept, only acquires meaning when it can be related to an idea already in the mind. For example, the word *magpie* only has meaning for an individual when it can be related to a mental representation of what magpies are. This knowledge can only be gained from a teacher (in the broadest sense of the word), and thus expository teaching is needed for learning to take place.

Ausubel termed the linking of new material to pre-existing concepts of **subsumption**, and suggested that it could take two forms: **derivative subsumption**, relating new information to previously learned highly similar concepts (owls are birds, therefore they can fly), and **correlative subsumption,** changing what is already known to allow it to relate to new information (ostriches are birds that cannot fly, therefore not all birds can fly). The result of learning, or subsumption, is a hierarchical structure of more or less organised and stable concepts, ranging from general principles at the top of the hierarchy to specific concepts at the bottom. This structure represents our understanding of the world.

the application of ausubel's approach to education

Like Bruner, Ausubel makes a number of recommendations for education. These include:

1. The use of **advance organisers**. These are a complex set of ideas given to learners before the material to be learned. A simple way of thinking of them is as introductory comments made by the teacher to alert the class to what they are going to learn during that lesson. The aim is to provide a cognitive structure to which new learning can be attached and to aid recall.
2. **Discriminability**. Ausubel argues that information which is similar to what is already known (derivative subsumption) is less likely to be remembered than information which is not that similar (correlative subsumption). Therefore a teacher should use techniques which highlight the differences between new material and pre-existing learning (to promote retention), as well as emphasising the similarities.
3. Making learning *meaningful*. Teachers should only teach material that the learner has been properly prepared to learn. In other words, before proceeding to teach a particular concept, the teacher should provide the learner with sufficient background information to make the understanding of that concept possible.

vygotsky's zone of proximal development: basic principles

Vygotsky's work centres on what he sees as the crucial role of culture and language in the development of human cognitive abilities. Culture can be defined as 'the physical, social, emotional, political, economic, artistic and spiritual environment in which we live, and the way that we interact with others both within and outside that environment' (Stapleton, 1993, p.1). According to Vygotsky, it is through these social interactions that we acquire language. With language comes knowledge of the culture in which we live and, at the same time, culture influences the language and knowledge that we acquire. As cultures change so does language and, therefore, thinking. Vygotsky saw knowledge of culture being passed on via language from adult to child, the adult being the experienced craftsperson who teaches the inexperienced apprentice that is the child.

Vygotsky believed that we are born with **elementary mental functions** such as attending and sensing, and that the pre-verbal infant is governed by these functions and is not capable of 'proper' thinking. Thought, or **higher mental functioning,** only comes with the acquisition of language. Vygotsky would thus argue that enhancing someone's language skills enhances their ability to think and therefore their understanding of the world. For the teacher then, the key to successful learning is providing learners with the language to deal with complex concepts.

the application of vygotsky's approach to education

In terms of applying Vygotsky's ideas about the role of culture and language to education, there are two important concepts that need to be considered: the *zone of proximal development (ZPD)* and *scaffolding*.

How good a job would you make of producing a CD by your favourite artist if you were put into a studio on your own tomorrow? How good a job would you do if you were given the assistance of a top producer? You'll probably agree that the results would be better if you have assistance than if you do not. This is basically what Vygotsky meant by the term zone of proximal development. The **zone of proximal development (ZPD)** is the difference between what a learner can achieve on their own and what they can achieve with help or instruction from a more experienced person.

Another way of thinking about the ZPD is that it is an individual's potential to learn. This way of looking at cognitive development takes into account individual differences. For example you may have a large potential for learning foreign languages, but your best friend or sibling may not. A teacher has to be aware of each learner's ZPD in order to be able to offer the right support at the right time and in order to maximise learning. One way of achieving this is through the use of a variety of assessment techniques that test the learners' understanding and ability.

Arising out of the concept of the ZPD and linked to the point made above is the notion of **scaffolding**. Scaffolding is a process in which, via language, a more competent person attempts to impart knowledge and understanding to a less competent person. It is more, however, than just instruction. The idea is that the teacher provides a framework within which learners are able to learn effectively for themselves.

For example, your teacher could easily instruct you on how to write an essay by dictating one to you. But you would not have learned anything from this. You would simply have followed the verbal instructions. In other words, your teacher's language would have controlled your behaviour. In order to have learned, you would have needed to have internalised the instructions and then self-regulated your own behaviour. So, instead of dictating an essay to you, your teacher would give you guidelines on HOW to write an essay (i.e. how an essay is structured, and what to include and exclude), but you would write the essay yourself. This way, the use of language allows you not only to learn about the content of the task, but also how to perform the task. Moreover, you have now acquired a transferable skill, that of writing essays, which you can apply to other subjects.

This process of communication via language between teacher and learner is sometimes referred to as **semiotic mediation**, and the shared understanding of a task that they come to as a result of this interaction is known as **intersubjectivity**. Without language, this intersubjectivity, this passing on of knowledge and the learning that accompanies it, would not occur, and the individual's ZPD would remain untouched.

Section summary **The application of the cognitive approach to education**
In this section we have considered the following:

- The cognitive view that human beings are information processors who develop schemas to help them understand the world and operate within it.
- Bruner's theory of discovery learning, with its view that humans construct their reality through the use of categories or coding systems. By understanding which mode of representation they use, teachers can explain any concept to any student. Teachers should revisit topics in increasing detail and complexity; this is known as the spiral curriculum.
- Ausubel's concepts of expository teaching and reception learning, in which students can be prepared for developing their skills of derivative and correlative subsumption by being given information directly by the teacher. This can be enhanced by the use of advance organisers and the development of discriminability.
- Vygotsky's insistence on the importance of culture in cognitive development and the crucial role of language in the shift from elementary to higher mental functioning. We also considered the application of these ideas via the concept of the zone of proximal development and the idea of scaffolding.

Humanistic applications to learning

INTRODUCTION

We have seen that in both the behaviourist and cognitive perspectives a scientific approach (in terms of the methods that they use and the theories that they generate) lies at the heart of each perspective. By way of contrast, the **humanistic** or **phenomenological approach**, as it is also referred to, is anti-scientific in the way that it investigates and considers human beings. The underpinning belief of this approach is that we are all *unique* individuals and, as such, there can be no *general* explanations or theories of human behaviour. We are all a product of our own particular set of circumstances and thus, in order to understand the individual we must understand that individual's subjective experience of what it is like to be them. (Atkinson, Atkinson, Smith and Bem, 1993).

Humanistic psychologists argue against the mechanistic qualities of the other perspectives. They reject the behaviourist theory that behaviour is controlled by external stimuli and the primary importance that cognitive psychologists place on information processing. They disagree with the fundamental belief that by applying certain processes to certain people at a certain time we can predict, and therefore control, their behaviour and their learning.

basic principles of humanism

One of the main proponents of the humanistic approach is Carl Rogers who, in his book *Client-Centred Therapy* (1951), put forward 19 propositions on the nature of human beings. Some of these are summarised in Table 4.2. From this table we can see that humanistic psychologists consider us to be proactive, unique individuals who exercise free will over our behaviour. We are who and what we are because that is what we have chosen for ourselves, and no one else can fully know us simply because of the fact that *they are not us*.

• **Table 4.2:** Major characteristics of human nature according to Rogers (1951) (adapted from Lefrancois (1997) p.243)

1. Reality is phenomenological.	Reality is what each individual conceives it to be. Therefore it is different for each of us and no one else can really know our reality.
2. Behaviour is motivated by the need to self-actualise.	We all have a deep-seated need to become the most complete human being we possibly can, and we spend our lives striving to achieve this goal.
3. Behaviour occurs within the context of personal realities.	The best way to understand another person is to try to see the world as they do. This means that we need effective, open, honest communication.
4. The self is constructed by the individual.	We learn who we are as the result of coming to terms with our experiences and combining them with the beliefs and attitudes that we have gained from others.
5. Our behaviours conform with our notions of self.	Generally speaking, we behave in ways that support the ideas we have about who and what we are.

This focus on the individual means that 'humanism objects to what is sometimes interpreted as the mechanistic, dehumanising, and inhumane emphases of "traditional" approaches to psychology and education. It urges adoption of new attitudes, concepts, and approaches in these fields' (Lefrancois, 1997, p.239). It is to these that we now turn.

the application of humanistic approaches to education

Given its focus on the whole individual, humanistic approaches to education are as much concerned with the development of the person as they are with the acquisition of knowledge. The word education derives from the Latin *ex ducere*, which means *to lead out*, and the aim of humanistic educational strategies is to lead out the potential of the student to assist them in their quest for self-actualisation. As was stated in Table 4.2, and as we shall see in Chapter 6, self-actualisation, becoming the most complete, *human*, human being you can is, according to humanistic psychologists, the ultimate motivator of human behaviour. How then do humanistic approaches affect what happens in the classroom? We shall consider two examples:

- learning styles
- process education.

learning styles

How do you do your homework? Alone in your bedroom in silence? With music on? Downstairs in the living room surrounded by your family? On the bus on the way to class? Do you require very explicit instructions or very minimal ones in order to complete tasks set by your teachers? Dunn and Griggs (1988) claim that the traditional education system works well for some but not so well for others. The fact that individuals learn best in different ways, at different times of the day, in different environments, suggests that each of us has a personal and unique **learning style**.

Traditional schools, however, often fail to recognise this and so the students who do best in this system are those whose learning style most closely matches the way the school is organised. Hour-long lessons on single subjects may be more easy to manage and organise, but they may not be suited to students with short attention spans who require frequent changes in stimulation. Similarly, a teacher-centred, instructional method – as advocated by Ausubel with his expository teaching approach described earlier in this chapter – will also fail to meet the learning requirements of some students.

Thus, within the traditional educational system, we have students who are more or less doomed to failure, not because of lack of ability or intelligence, but simply because they are not educated in the manner which best suits them as an individual.

All is not lost, as schools may, and some do, attempt to adapt themselves to the learning styles of their students, and the characteristics of a more humanistic approach to the actual teaching of students is outlined in Table 4.3. It is unlikely, however, that many schools will be able to adopt a fully humanistic approach as is advocated here, because of the pressure of finances and other resources.

• **Table 4.3:** The major characteristics of a learning styles-driven school (after Lefrancois, 1997)

What needs to be done	How this can be achieved
1. Students must be profiled on entry to determine their learning style	Through the use of such inventories as Renzulli and Smith's (1978) Learning Styles Inventory or Gregorc's (1982) Style Delineator. These are both forms of questionnaires concerned with how students learn.
2. Students must be given choice over the learning environment.	By providing a range of different settings, such as individual study rooms, rooms with soft carpets for lying on to work, group-working rooms and so on.
3. Students must be given choice over when they learn.	By rotating subjects so that the same lesson is offered at various times in the week, including early morning and late afternoon.
4. Students should have control over the assessment schedule.	Exams and coursework should be taken when the student is ready, not according to some pre-determined timetable.
5. Students should be fully involved in the organisation of the school.	By having effective school councils with a large number of student representatives rather than just token student members.
6. The school should put equal emphasis on creativity and problem-solving, and not just on the end product (exam results).	By ensuring student involvement at all times and awarding creativity and problem-solving as well as academic achievement.

process education

Rogers argues for a humanistic approach that is centred around problem-solving and builds on the natural potentials of the student. He argues that students are eager to develop and learn, and that this desire for knowledge and understanding should provide the basis of the education system. In order to capitalise on this natural potential to learn, subject matter should be relevant, self-evaluation should be encouraged and the student should be made to feel safe and secure. Learning from doing (experiential learning) rather than instruction should be promoted and the student should be supported in the development of their independence, creativity and self-reliance. In this way, the education system would equip students with the essential tool needed for modern life: the ability to live comfortably with change (Rogers, 1969).

This approach focuses very much on the *process* of education, that is on how education is to take place, rather than on the product, what is learned and how is it assessed. As such it has major implications for the role of the teacher, who Rogers sees as a *facilitator* of learning rather than an *instructor* in knowledge. Rogers termed this approach **process education**. Consequently, he proposed a set of guidelines for the teacher-as-facilitator which included teachers seeing themselves as resources to be used as and when the students need them, sharing thoughts and feelings with students in an open and accepting way, becoming participant learners and acknowledging their own limitations. The extent to which Rogers' ideas have been taken up by teachers is limited. Very few have wholeheartedly taken on board the entire range of the humanistic approach, but many utilise at least some aspects of it in their day to day teaching (Lefrancois, 1994).

It is worth noting, however, that the majority of educational systems actively work against the incorporation of the humanistic approach, since the majority of people working within the system do not subscribe to humanistic values. They argue that the failure of so-called 'free schools' (of which Summerhill is the best known example in the UK) to match the exam results of the more traditional schools indicates the weakness of the humanistic approach. Proponents of the humanistic approach, however, would point out that this misses the point completely. Education is not just about exam results, it is about developing the student's potential, and simply being well-qualified does not necessarily make someone a better human being.

Section summary   **The application of the humanistic approach to education**

In the final section of this chapter on applying psychological perspectives to education we considered:

- The humanistic view of human nature: the idea that we are unique individuals with free will and our own phenomenology. We also considered some of the main points proposed by Carl Rogers about the nature of humanity.
- Two applications of the humanistic approach: learning styles, with its argument that the educational system should fit the student, rather than the student fit the system, and process education, which suggests that it is the process of development as human beings which should be the focus of education, not the mere acquisition of knowledge.

The reductionism versus holism debate is concerned with whether or not a complex phenomenon like human behaviour can best be explained by investigating it in its entirety (holism) or by examining it in its component parts (reductionism).

Humanistic psychology, with its emphasis on the complete, complex human being comes down very much on the holistic side of this debate. Supporters of this approach argue that since human life is neither lived nor experienced in discreet little packages, any attempt to understand it must inevitably deal with the complex interrelationships within which it occurs.

Behaviourists and cognitivists, on the other hand, would argue that you can explain all human behaviour by reference to relatively straightforward underlying principles, and to that extent they take a reductionist approach. For behaviourists these principles are the laws of learning and, therefore in order to explain human behaviour you simply need to uncover the chain of stimulus response units that has led to the behaviour itself. Since behaviourists consider human behaviour to be the result of the same processes that determine the behaviour of far less complex organisms, such as rats, pigeons and even cockroaches, the type of reductionism that behaviourists employ is termed biological reductionism.

While sharing the behaviourists' belief in reductionist principles, cognitive psychologists see the underlying cause of human behaviour as being the way we process, 'misprocess', or fail to process information. Cognitive psychologists often use the computer analogy for human beings and liken human behaviour to computer programmes. They are therefore said to subscribe to machine reductionism.

Which of these approaches is most valid is a matter of ongoing discussion. It could be argued that they all have a role to play, depending on what the investigation into human behaviour is hoping to achieve. For instance, if we simply want to understand how school phobia comes about, or we want to remove it relatively quickly then biological and machine reductionism can provide us with solutions. If, however, we want to explain to parents of children with school phobia what their children are experiencing then the more holistic approach of humanistic psychology would seem more appropriate.

KEY TERMS

behaviourism; classical conditioning; unconditioned stimulus; conditioned stimulus; unconditioned response; conditioned response; extinction; systematic desensitisation; operant conditioning; law of effect; positive reinforcement; negative reinforcement; punishment; behaviour shaping; programmed learning; extinction; discrimination; cognitive schemas; discovery learning: constructivism; spiral curriculum; mode of representation; enactive; iconic; symbolic; expository teaching: reception learning; subsumption; derivative subsumption; correlative subsumption; advanced organisers; discriminability; zone of proximal development; elementary mental functions; higher mental functioning; scaffolding; semiotic mediation; intersubjectivity; humanism; learning styles; process education.

EXERCISES

- Would you like to attend a 'Free School', where you decide what, when and how to learn? Discuss this with your classmates.
- Do you need rewards (reinforcement) in order to do your work? What are those rewards? Who provides them? Which type is most effective?
- Compare your learning style with that of your classmates. What are the strengths and weaknesses of the different styles?

1 (a) Describe one application of the cognitive perspective to education.
   (b) Discuss the advantages and disadvantages of using this application in the classroom.

2 (a) Outline behaviourist applications to education.
   (b) Compare and contrast behaviourist applications with applications from other perspectives.

3 (a) Describe applications of psychological perspectives to education.
   (b) Evaluate the application of psychological perspectives to education.
   (c) Giving reasons for your answer, suggest how you would design a classroom using humanistic principles.

Further reading

Atkinson, R. L., Atkinson, R. C., Smith, E. E. & Bem, D. J. (1993) *Introduction to Psychology* (11th ed). Fort Worth, TX: Harcourt Brace Jovanovitch.
Provides a good basic introduction to the main psychological perspectives.

Lefrancois, G. R. (1994) *Psychology for Teaching* (8th ed). Belmont, CA: Wadsworth.
Gives a very readable account of the application of the behaviourist, cognitive and humanistic approaches to education.

Websites

http://cstl-cla.semo.edu/snell/py101
Home page of Dr. Snell of Southeast Missouri State University, with powerpoint presentations and lecture notes on perspectives in psychology.

http://campus.houghton.edu/depts/psychology/lrn2/
A series of slides on perspectives in psychology.

http://www.psywww.com/index.html
An American site full of information about psychology, including links to the APA (American Psychological Association).

Learning styles and teaching styles

Introduction

In many ways, learning styles and teaching styles are two sides of the same coin. Learning styles are concerned with how learners learn while teaching styles refer to how teachers teach, and the two obviously interact with each other in the classroom and affect both the quality and quantity of learning that takes place (Bennett, 1976). It is rare, however, that the preferred learning style of *all* the students in a class and the preferred teaching style of the teacher coincide.

In this chapter we will consider the following topics:

- Definitions, theories and measurement of learning and teaching styles
- Individual differences in learning styles
- Improving learning effectiveness (study skills).

Definitions, theories and measurement of learning and teaching styles

DEFINITIONS AND THEORIES OF LEARNING STYLES

Kolb (1984) defines learning style as a student's reasonably consistent response to and use of stimuli in an educational context. In other words, a student's learning style is the combination of the behaviours that they engage in when learning. Kolb also points out that any individual's learning style is a result of the interaction of heredity, past experience and present environment, and as such is not necessarily a fixed and static construct.

Leith (1974), for example, showed that personality was related very strongly to students' preferred learning styles. Having measured students' personalities using Eysenck's Personality Inventory (EPI), Leith arranged for them to study a course on genetics via discovery and instructional learning. Leith found that extroverts learnt better (as measured by a class test) when engaged in collaborative learning, compared to introverts who performed better when working alone. However, both could learn reasonably effectively when utilising their non-preferred learning style.

There have been numerous attempts to classify learning styles, but only two will be considered here. These two have been chosen, not because they are the most important, but because between them they encompass most of the learning styles that have been identified. These are:

*   Curry's 'onion model' of learning styles
*   Grasha's six learning styles.

curry's 'onion model' of learning styles

As the name suggests, Curry's (1983) **onion model** uses the analogy of an onion to categorise and describe learning styles. In this model, there are three layers, each characterised by different influences on the learning process and varying in their degree of stability (see Figure 5.1).

The outer layer, which Curry refers to as **instructional preference**, is the student's preference for ways of learning and being taught, and here the major

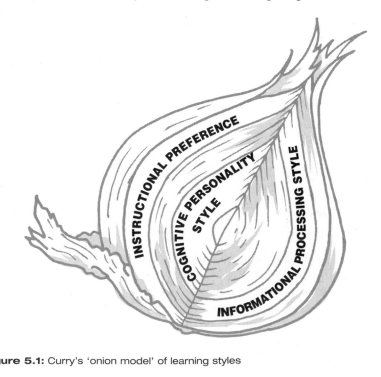

•   **Figure 5.1:** Curry's 'onion model' of learning styles

influences come from the learning environment. Variables such as teacher and parental expectations, teaching style, the physical environment of the classroom and so on can affect instructional preference, and this makes this the most unstable of the three learning styles, or layers, that comprise Curry's onion model.

The middle layer is labelled the **informational processing style** and focuses on the strategies that students use to process information. Gagne (1985, p.33) defines these cognitive strategies as 'goal-directed sequences of cognitive operations that lead from the student's comprehension of a question or instructions to the answer or other requested performance'. This style, whilst still open to influence by others (such as how clearly the teacher explains the task to be undertaken) is more stable than the outer layer of instructional preference.

The final layer, which is the most stable of the three learning styles identified by Curry, is the **cognitive personality style** and reflects the student's underlying approach to thinking. Some of us seem to be lateral or divergent thinkers, which means that we explore problems from a number of different avenues at the same time before coming to a solution (indeed, we may offer a number of solutions). Others of us are vertical or convergent thinkers, focus on a single aspect of a problem and do not move on until we have resolved that aspect. In addition, this layer also takes into account the way that:

> our deepest personality traits shape the orientations we take toward the world. The popular **Myers-Briggs Type Indicators** [a learning-style inventory] categorises people as extroverts/introverts, sensing/intuition, thinking/feeling, and judging/perceiving. How individuals rate along these scales indicates tendencies in their attitudes toward engaging with the world. [Curry's onion model] … anchors our preferences in our very make-up (O'Connor, 1997, p.3).

In other words, Curry argues that the core of our learning style is shaped by our personality. Table 5.1 outlines the main characteristics of the Myers-Briggs Type Indicator referred to above.

It could be argued that we all possess the three 'onion' layers, but to differing degrees, and this contributes to our own unique learning style. Those of us who have a relatively strong centre to our onion, as it were, are much less flexible in our approach to learning than someone with a cognitive personality style that is not as rigid. Those of us with a more eclectic learning preference are more likely to be able to cope with learning in a variety of settings and via a number of different approaches. We would also be more amenable to utilising a range of learning strategies or study skills than others.

Perhaps what is most important about Curry's model is that it implies that, whilst learning style may be more or less fixed, we can still acquire a range of strategies that can improve the effectiveness of the way that we learn – although this may be easier for some than others.

• **Table 5.1:** The learning styles of the Myers-Briggs Type Indicators and their main characteristics (based on Felder, 1996)

Learning style dimension	Main features
Extrovert or Introvert (E or I)	Extroverts: active, like to try things out, focus on outer world of people Introverts: passive, think things through, focus on inner world of ideas
Sensors or Intuitors (S or N)	Sensors: practical, detail-oriented, focus on facts and procedures Intuitors: imaginative, concept-oriented, focus on meanings and possibilities
Thinkers or Feelers (T or F)	Thinkers: sceptical, decisions based on logic and rules Feelers: appreciative, decisions made on personal and humanistic considerations
Judgers or Perceivers (J or P)	Judgers: set and follow agendas, seek closure even with incomplete data Perceivers: adapt to changing circumstances, resist closure to obtain more data
Note: These learning style dimensions or preferences can be combined to form 16 different learning style types, e.g. ESTJ and INFJ are two types.	

grasha's six learning styles

Grasha (1996) has suggested **six categories of learning style** (see Table 5.2) that he believes we all possess to a greater or lesser extent. Ideally, a student would be able to draw upon all of these styles, choosing the ones most appropriate to the tasks in hand. In reality, most of us tend to rely on one or two and rarely, if ever, utilise the other approaches to learning that Grasha identifies.

An awareness of the existence of more than one learning style should encourage students to develop a range of study habits that they can use to maximise learning, while at the same time it challenges teachers to manage the curriculum to allow a range of learning styles to be used. It would also be argued by humanistic psychologists that teachers should encourage students to pursue personal growth and development in their underused learning styles as part of their journey towards self-actualisation.

• **Table 5.2:** Grasha's six learning styles

Learning style	Description of typical behaviours associated with the learning style
Independent	Independent, self-paced study; preference for working alone on coursework projects
Dependent	Looks to teacher and fellow students for guidance and structure; prefers to be told what to do by an authority figure
Competitive	Motivated by desire to do better than other students; likes recognition for academic achievement
Collaborative	Co-operates with teacher and fellow students; prefers small-group discussions and group projects
Avoidant	Unenthusiastic about and uninterested in learning; sometimes overwhelmed by class activities and often absent
Participant	Interested in class activities and eager to work; aware of and shows desire to meet teacher's expectations

DEFINITIONS AND THEORIES OF TEACHING STYLES

All of us have our favourite teachers, but what is it about them that makes them a good teacher? What is it about the way they teach us that lights that spark of enthusiasm in us? Perhaps one answer to these questions lies in their *teaching style*, what Lefrancois (1997, p.220) calls 'an identifiable and related group of teaching activities'. This definition is in itself, however, not enough. We need to be able to identify and compare different teaching styles in order to consider the effect they may have on learning. After all, if the teaching style used has no impact on the learning that takes place, then why is a great deal of time, effort and money spent on training teachers?

What, then are the different teaching styles we are likely to come across? The answer to this is more complex than it may at first appear. Some researchers identify very specific methods of instructing, including the lecturing style, the seminar style and so on. Others identify less specific approaches which focus on the teacher–student relationship, such as the authoritarian style, and the laissez-faire style. Still others consider much more broadly-based classifications such as formal and informal teaching styles.

To confuse the picture even further, we have to accept that a single teacher may adopt any one or more of these teaching styles depending on the circumstances. For example, if a teacher has a class of 80 A level psychology students then a formal lecturing style would be most appropriate. If, however, the class is a small group of foundation students with learning difficulties, and the subject is personal and social education, then a more informal teaching approach would be more successful. Thus, the teaching style adopted by the teacher will be affected by such concerns as who the students are, how many of them there are in the class, the subject matter being covered and the objectives of the lesson.

A variety of other factors such as the experience and personality of the teacher, the training they have undergone, the textbooks and other resources that they have access to, the amount of preparation they are able to do and so on, will also have an influence on the teaching style they adopt. Having said that, it is nonetheless true that most teachers tend to use one particular habitual style most of the time.

We are not concerned here with different methods of instruction such as the formal lecture or the informal discussion, but rather with the broader categorisations of teaching styles. Two approaches to classifying teaching styles will be considered:

- Formal–informal teaching style
- High initiative–low initiative teaching style.

formal–informal teaching style

Based on empirical research, Bennett (1976) drew up a typology or classification of teaching styles and identified them as either **formal** or **informal**. A formal teaching style is one in which the teacher is very much in control. It is the teacher who decides what is to be taught, how it is to be taught, the layout of the classroom and, even, the seating arrangements of the students. This *teacher-centred approach* is often considered to be the *traditional* method of teaching. By way of contrast, the informal approach involves much more *negotiation* between the students and the teachers about how learning is to be undertaken, the nature and form of assessment and so on. In other words, it is much more *student-* or *learner-centred*.

Bennett's original research suggests that the formal approach is more effective than the informal approach, at least among school children and when the material being learnt is academic in nature. Students who were taught by teachers using a formal teaching style consistently outperformed those who had an informal teaching style in English and Mathematics, with the exception of one class who, despite having an informal teacher, fared better than most.

Bennett suggested that this anomalous result could be explained by the fact that although the teacher was informal in her style of teaching, she was still highly organised and well-prepared, extremely good at motivating her students, and structured her lessons effectively. Thus it is important to note that an informal teaching style does not necessarily mean a disorganised, unprepared teacher!

high initiative–low initiative teaching style

Fontana (1995) describes an alternative way of classifying teaching styles based on the work that Leikart and his colleagues have done with young children. This is the **high initiative–low initiative** classification and Fontana points out that these should not be confused with formal and informal styles. He argues that 'a high initiative teacher can operate in both formal and informal contexts' (Fontana, 1995, p. 389) but will show the same fundamental characteristics in both.

The characteristics of a high initiative teacher are shown in Table 5.3. Those of a low initiative teacher are the opposite of those detailed in this table. Fontana points out that 'high initiative teachers tend to have high initiative children, and even in highly curriculum-based situations are able to develop initiative-driven work' (Fontana, 1995, p. 389). By implication, the opposite is true of low initiative teachers.

■ **Table 5.3:** Characteristics of a high initiative teacher (after Fontana, 1995)

Characteristic	Effect on teaching
Aware of the needs of individual students	Varies learning tasks to address these needs
Willing to learn from students	Uses relevant, task-centred, appropriate questions
Allows students to make full use of their skills and abilities	Uses a variety of tasks which challenge and stretch students
Allows students to make informed choices	Manages the curriculum in a flexible and stimulating way
Encourages the development of self-confidence, independence and responsibility in students	Allows students to make decisions and sets up problem-solving activities

Having briefly considered definitions and types of teaching and learning styles, we will now turn our attention to the perennial problem of measuring learning, and the associated concepts of reliability and validity.

MEASURING LEARNING STYLES AND TEACHING STYLES

It should be obvious from some of the language used to describe learning and teaching styles, including words such as 'preferences' and 'initiative', that we are dealing with fairly abstract cognitive events. This means that in order to identify which style someone uses, or measure the extent to which they use one style over another, we have to ask them questions. Students and teachers are given questionnaires, inventories and scales to complete about their learning and teaching behaviours, and are classified on the basis of their responses as using a particular learning or teaching style.

Before we look at some examples of these inventories, it is important to consider why anyone would want to measure learning and teaching styles – if there were no purpose to the measurement then it would be a waste of time doing it! There are as many ways of measuring learning and teaching styles as there are types, but they all share the same goal, that of reliably and validly assessing the effectiveness of different styles.

In their meta-analysis of gender differences in learning orientations, Severiens and ten Dam (1998) point out that there are a wide range of instruments which measure learning styles. These include the Approaches to Studying Inventory (ASI) (Entwistle, 1981), the Inventory of Learning Processes (ILP) (Schmeck, 1983), the Study Behaviour Questionnaire (SBQ) (Biggs, 1987), and the Study Process Questionnaire (SPQ) (Biggs, 1987). We will now consider two examples of learning and teaching styles inventories in order to grasp the underlying principles involved in their construction and their use. These are:

- Entwistle's Approaches to Studying Inventory (ASI)
- Kyriacou and Wilkins' measurement of teacher-centred and student-centred teaching styles.

entwistle's approaches to studying inventory (asi)

Developed in 1981, the **Approaches to Studying Inventory (ASI)** is made up of 64 Likert-type items organised into 16 scales. A Likert scale is one in which the respondent has to rate a series of characteristics on a numerical scale. For example: on a scale of 1 to 7 (with 1 meaning 'very difficult' and 7 meaning 'very easy'), how would you rate your ability to understand this topic? The 16 scales of the ASI are then further categorised into groups ranging from 2 to 6 in number to yield four learning orientations: the Reproducing, Meaning, Achieving and Non-academic Orientations. Table 5.4 outlines the major characteristics of each of these learning orientations and their associated scales.

In order to complete the ASI students simply rate themselves for each of the 64 Likert-type items and thus gain a score for each item. These are then added together to determine a score for each of the 16 scales and from these the student can calculate which learning orientation they use most frequently.

• **Table 5.4:** Scales of the Approaches to Studying Inventory (adapted from Severiens and ten Dam 1998)

Scale	Meaning
Meaning Orientation	
Deep approach	Uses active questioning in learning
Use of evidence	Is able to relate evidence to conclusions
Inter-relating ideas	Relates current topic to other parts of the course
Comprehension learning	Readiness to map out subject area and think divergently
Operation learning	Emphasis on facts and logical analysis
Intrinsic motivation	Interested in learning for its own sake
Reproducing Orientation	
Surface approach	Displays a preoccupation with memorisation
Syllabus-boundness	Relies on teacher to define learning tasks
Improvidence	Over-cautious reliance on details
Fear of failure	Pessimism and anxiety about academic outcomes
Achieving Orientation	
Strategic approach	Aware of implications of academic demands made by teacher
Achievement motivation	Competitive and confident
Non-academic Orientation	
Disorganised study methods	Unable to work regularly and effectively
Negative attitudes to studying	Lack of interest and application
Globetrotting	Over-ready to jump to conclusions
Extrinsic motivation	Interested in courses for the qualifications they offer

This practice of rating inventory items is common to many measures of learning and teaching styles and allows a quantitative measurement to be taken. The advantage of this, as Severiens and ten Dam (1998) have shown, is that it allows for statistical analysis of individual differences in learning and teaching styles.

It can be seen from Table 5.4 that several of the items in the ASI are very similar to some of the learning styles proposed by Curry and Grasha. Entwistle's *Meaning Orientation* and *Achieving Orientation* reflect Curry's middle and outer layers respectively, whilst the syllabus-boundness of the Reproducing Orientation and the qualities displayed in the Non-academic Orientation are equivalent to Grasha's dependent and avoidant learning styles. These similarities emphasise the point that, although many definitions and types of learning styles have been identified, they are all subtle variations on a theme.

a measurement of teacher-centred and student-centred teaching styles

In a study carried out in 1993, Kyriacou and Wilkins set out to discover whether or not the introduction of guidelines on teaching the National Curriculum published by the Department for Education and Employment had actually had an effect on the way that teachers taught.

As part of this study they measured the degree to which teachers employed either a teacher-centred (what Bennett would have termed formal) style or student-centred (informal) teaching style. Table 5.5 shows 9 of the 20 inventory items that they used. To complete this inventory, teachers were required to place a tick under one of the five central columns that reflected their teaching practice in relation to each of the bipolar statements contained in the inventory.

The bipolar items themselves are a kind of expanded semantic differential scale (Osgood *et al.*, 1957 in Gross, 1996). Phrases of opposite meaning, rather than single words of opposite meaning, are used and the respondent simply has to indicate towards which end of the scale their behaviour lies. As with Entwistle's ASI, this produces a score that is then used to classify the teaching style.

As well as providing a good example of a measuring instrument for teaching styles, the Kyriacou and Wilkins study also shows us that teachers can alter their style as a result of external influences: they reported that the majority of teachers in their study had moved towards a more student-centred style since the introduction of the National Curriculum.

• **Table 5.5:** Some of the bipolar items used to measure teacher-centred and student-centred teaching styles (adapted from Kyriacou and Wilkins, 1993)

Statement X	X	Tend to X	0	Tend to Y	Y	Statement Y
Activities carried out by pupils are restricted to those set out by the teacher						Activities carried out by pupils are variable and negotiated with the teacher
Pupil activities are mainly writing and listening						Pupil activities are mainly problem-solving and experimental
The main activity of the teacher is to lecture and provide information						The main activity of the teacher is to facilitate and enable pupils to learn
The teacher's role is fixed, being a provider						The teacher's role varies, being enabler and facilitator
Resources are limited in number and variety						Resources are numerous and varied
The time spent on activities is fixed, being determined by the teacher						The time spent on activities is variable and flexible, being negotiated by the pupil with the teacher
The classroom has a formal layout which rarely changes						The layout of the classroom is flexible, changing according to the activities going on
The objectives of lessons are usually content based						Process is the main objective of lessons
Assessment is normally under the control of the teacher						Both pupil and teacher have a say in assessment

Whenever we measure anything we need to be sure that the instrument we are using measures what it claims to measure (**validity**) and that it is consistent (**reliability**).

To assess the validity of measures of learning and teaching styles (or measures of any other behaviour, come to that), we can do a number of things. Firstly, we can subject the inventories to the 'eyeball test' – that is, we look at them. If from the way the items are written they seem to be measuring what they claim to be measuring, then we can say they have *face validity*. Is this true of the inventories described in this chapter?

Secondly, we can compare the results of the inventory with the results of another inventory that is already known to be valid. If there is a high correlation between them (for the same participants) then we can say they have *concurrent validity*, because the results of the two inventories agree or concur with each other.

Thirdly, we can give the inventories to two groups of people who are known to differ in learning styles and, if the inventory shows this difference, then we know that it has *construct validity*.

Finally, we can use the score obtained on the inventory to predict the future behaviour of the participant. If they behave in line with what their inventory score suggests their behaviour will be, then the inventory has *predictive validity*.

We also need to know whether or not an inventory is consistent and reliable. Firstly, we need to know whether or not all the test items are measuring the same thing. In other words, is the measure internally consistent or reliable? We can test for this in two ways: either by writing two versions of the inventory and comparing scores for the same people on each (if they agree then the test has *parallel forms reliability*) or by comparing scores on one half of the test with scores on the other half for the same person(s) (if these agree then the inventory has *split-half reliability*).

Secondly, we need to know about the consistency of the inventory over time. If a group of students are given a learning styles questionnaire in January then, if it is consistent over time, they should get more or less the same result if they complete the same questionnaire six months later. If they do, then the inventory has *test – re-test reliability*.

Finally a word of warning. If a measuring instrument is valid (i.e. measures what it claims to measure) then it will be reliable (i.e. it will give consistent measurements). However, if a measuring instrument is reliable, this does not automatically mean that it is valid, because it could be consistently measuring the wrong thing!

Definitions, theories and measurement of learning and teaching styles

In this section we have considered the following:

- it is possible to define learning styles in a number of ways and various models of learning styles exist
- Curry's onion model consists of three interactive layers: instructional preference, information processing style and cognitive personality style. The degree to which we possess each of these three dimensions determines our own unique learning style
- Grasha proposes six learning styles: independent, dependent, competitive, collaborative, avoidant and participant. Each is characterised by its own set of related behaviours and motivations
- there are numerous definitions of teaching style, but the one thing they all have in common is that they focus on the teacher's preferred way of teaching
- Bennett's informal and formal teaching styles are based on empirical research, and relate to the approach that the teacher takes towards the student
- Fontana's model of high initiative and low initiative teachers highlights the main characteristics of each style, and the effects these have on teaching
- the reason for measuring learning and teaching styles is to provide students and teachers with information about their learning and teaching behaviours. This then puts them in a better position to adopt other styles if they need/choose to
- Entwistle's Approaches to Studying Inventory (ASI) was described and the links between this and Grasha's six learning styles was identified
- Kyriacou and Wilkins' teacher-centred/student-centred inventory was described, and its development out of the National Curriculum was noted
- the Theme Link considered the issues of the reliability and validity of measurement.

Individual differences in learning styles

At the beginning of this chapter we considered two models of learning styles, Curry's onion model and Grasha's six learning styles. Both models make implicit claims that there are individual differences in learning styles. If you look back at Table 5.1, for example, it is possible to conclude that possessing different combinations of Grasha's six categories contributes to each individual's unique learning style. The purpose of this section is to take a slightly wider approach to individual differences by considering learning styles in relation to gender and culture as well. Thus this section will cover the following three topics:

- individual differences
- gender differences
- cultural differences.

INDIVIDUAL DIFFERENCES

According to Felder (1996, p.18) students have:

> characteristic strengths and preferences in the ways they take in and process information. Some students tend to focus on facts, data and algorithms; others are more comfortable with theories and mathematical models. Some respond strongly to visual forms of information, like pictures, diagrams and schematics; others get more from verbal forms – written and spoken explanations. Some prefer to learn actively and interactively; others function more introspectively and individually.

This means, of course, that students' learning styles will have an impact on their educational performance, particularly if those learning styles are at odds with the information being presented or the teaching style being used.

Yokomoto (cited in Felder, 1996) showed that an individual student's learning style was closely related to his progress on an introductory course in electrical circuits. Yokomoto uses the Myer-Briggs Type Indicator (MBTI) as a diagnostic tool with students who are having difficulties with their studies. One such student, who was identified as an ISTJ (introvert, sensor, thinker, judger) learner, and who was failing an introductory course in electrical engineering, was found to be relying too much on memorisation and repetition (characteristics of ISTJ learners) as a way of problem-solving. Yokomoto supported the student in developing other approaches based more on understanding the concepts involved in the subject and that student actually went on to achieve a master's degree. Similarly, an ENTJ (extrovert, intuitor, thinker, judger) student showed improved performance when he was shown that the use of routine procedures (a characteristic of sensors rather than intuitors) allowed him to complete some tasks more easily than his usual style did, thus freeing up time for further study.

Schroeder (2001) has also found that students who differ on the MBTI tend to show differential educational performance. For example, students categorised as introvert/intuitive learners have significantly higher SATs scores, perform better across a range of standardised timed aptitude tests and achieve higher grades in the first year of their degree courses than do those categorised as extrovert/sensing learners. Schroeder also points out that differences in learning styles play a part in subject choice at university. ES students are dominant in business, nursing and other health courses, whilst IN learners are disproportionately represented in science and arts courses.

GENDER DIFFERENCES

As mentioned earlier, Severiens and ten Dam (1998) carried out a meta-analysis of research into gender differences in learning styles. This means that they analysed the results of a number of other studies (22 in all) to find out whether or not the differences that these other studies reported were consistent. The 22 studies that they analysed had all been conducted using the ASI to measure learning style. Severiens and ten Dam then explored, via statistical analysis, whether the findings of the original studies reflected gender preferences for different learning styles, or other variables in the way those studies were conducted.

They reported the following gender differences. Women scored higher than men on the Reproduction Orientation but lower on the Non-academic Orientation. This suggests that female students are more dependent on teachers and have a greater fear of failure than male students, but are keener to learn, can work more regularly and more effectively, and have a more positive attitude to studying than their male counterparts. There were no significant differences between the genders on either the Meaning Orientation or the Achieving Orientation, which suggests that both genders can be competitive, confident, logical and analytical.

At the same time, however, they found gender differences on 11 of the 16 scales (e.g. relating ideas, fear of failure, negative attitude to studying) that comprise the four learning orientations of the ASI. This apparent contradiction in the results can be explained as a result of factors other than gender, such as intelligence, age, educational experiences and types of learning tasks.

It would seem, therefore, that there *are* gender differences in learning styles, but we have to be careful to take into account the possibility that gender alone may not be the reason for these differences.

CULTURAL DIFFERENCES

When considering cultural differences in learning styles, Sadler-Smith and Tsang (1998) describe the 'perception of Asian students by Australian and expatriate teachers as one of rote learners characterised by memorisation, fragmentation, "regurgitation" and a lack of insight and understanding' (p.83). They suggest, however, that much of this characterisation of Asian students is based on stereotyping, and cite research by Biggs (1987, 1989) and Kember and Gow (1990) comparing Hong Kong students with Australian students. Research by Watkins, Reghi and Astilla (1991) on Filipino and Nepalese children also shows that the stereotype is false. It is worth noting here that Sadler-Smith and Tsang's use of the term 'Asian students' refers to those students from Chinese, Japanese, Malaysian, Filipino and other similar backgrounds. It does not include those from Indian, Pakistani, Bangladeshi or Sri Lankan backgrounds as it would if used in the UK, and so, once again, we must be wary of generalisations.

Using a revised version of the ASI (the RASI), Sadler-Smith and Tsang compared the learning styles of students from Hong Kong with those from the UK and found that it was the British students who relied most on memorisation. At the same time, however, the UK students showed a deeper approach (equivalent to the Meaning Orientation on the original version of the ASI described previously) 'perhaps suggesting that the UK students had adopted a "deep memorisation" [or memorisation with meaning as Tang (1997) defines it] approach, that is they had accepted the intrinsic value of learning and the ... academic values of the institution but were combining this with memorisation as a strategy to meet the demands of assessment systems in their institution' (Sadler-Smith and Tsang, 1998, p.89).

Sadler-Smith and Tsang also point out that the differences they found may have been due to the somewhat unrepresentative nature of the UK sample (225 business studies students), the limitations of the RASI as a measurement tool in a non-Western culture, or the possibility that memorisation in Hong Kong should be regarded as a separate factor since it is seen there as a precursor and adjunct to understanding rather than inferior to it.

This study indicates that we must be very cautious in drawing conclusions about cultural differences in learning style. There may well be differences there, but they may be relatively minor, run counter to anecdotal evidence and popular conceptions, be the result of the use of culturally limited measuring instruments or culturally bound concepts, such as the nature of memorisation.

Section summary   **Individual differences in learning styles**

In this section we considered evidence about the nature of individual differences in learning style in relation to gender and culture. We have seen, therefore, that:

- individual differences in learning style are related to educational performance
- if students are made aware of this and supported in developing additional learning styles, their performance can improve
- subject choice may also be influenced by learning style
- gender differences in learning style do exist and can be measured by using the Approaches to Studying Inventory described earlier. On the ASI, women were found to score higher on the reproduction orientation and lower on the non-academic orientation than their male counterparts
- measuring cultural differences in learning styles is more problematic due to stereotyping, the possibility of ethnocentrism in the ASI, and other such factors.

Improving learning effectiveness (study skills)

As has been shown, whilst we all have preferred methods or styles of learning, these are not entirely fixed and may change over time or in relation to the task to be done. This suggests, also, that there are numerous strategies that we can 'bolt on' to our habitual style in order to improve the effectiveness of our learning. Broadly speaking, these strategies can be categorised into three groups: those that aim at matching teaching styles to learning styles, those that focus on specific aspects of learning, and those that are concerned with learning about how we learn. We will look at one example from each of these three categories:

- McCarthy's 4-MAT system
- The PQRST method
- The Spelt approach.

MATCHING TEACHING STYLES TO LEARNING STYLES: MCCARTHY'S 4-MAT SYSTEM

The obvious strategy here would be for teachers to give each of their students a learning styles inventory to complete and, from the results of that survey, to plan their lessons accordingly. They could then ensure that at least part of every lesson was conducted in a way that matches the variety of learning styles present in the students.

One way of achieving this is for teachers to implement **McCarthy's 4-MAT system** (1990) of lesson planning. In the first stage, *motivation*, students are asked to individually draw up a lesson plan for the topic to be covered, what McCarthy called *creating the experience* and then *reflecting on the experience* by sharing their ideas with others in small groups.

The second stage, or *concept development*, is where the students' own lesson plans are discussed in relation to the topic (*integration of reflections into concepts*) prior to relevant content being provided, either directly by the teacher or via the use of handouts and textbooks (*presentation and development of theories and concepts*).

The third stage is that of *practice*. Here students are required to carry out practical activities and exercises in order to develop further understanding of the content. This allows them to *practise and reinforce new information* and to *personalise the experience*.

The final stage, *application*, involves students in applying the knowledge they have gained to a novel situation by *developing a plan for applying new concepts*. The final stage is *doing it and sharing it with others*, which involves discussing ideas in small groups.

Table 5.6 shows how some of the learning styles identified by Grasha and by the ASI would also be addressed by using the 4-MAT approach to lesson planning. Whilst not all learning styles are satisfied using this approach, it does ensure that the majority of students are able to spend at least some of the lesson learning in their preferred style.

● **Table 5.6:** How McCarthy's 4-MAT system of lesson planning meets the needs of most of the learning styles identified by Grasha and by Entwistle's ASI

Component of McCarthy's 4-MAT system	Grasha's learning styles	ASI learning styles
Motivation	Collaborative participant	Meaning orientation
Concept development	Dependent	Reproducing orientation
Practice	Competitive	Achieving orientation
Application	Independent	Meaning orientation

Another advantage of this approach is that students are given the opportunity to experience learning styles other than their preferred one. They may even discover that for some of the tasks an alternative way of learning is better than their usual method.

THE PQRST METHOD FOR LEARNING FROM TEXTBOOKS

Atkinson *et al.* (1993) state that the **PQRST method** 'is intended to improve a student's ability to study and remember material presented in a textbook (Thomas and Robinson, 1982). The method takes its name from the first letters of its five stages: *Preview, Question, Read, Self-recitation,* and *Test*' (p.321). The PQRST method is suitable for use with most learning styles, and particularly for the collaborative, participant and independent learning styles identified by Grasha. It is summarised in Table 5.7 below.

● **Table 5.7:** A summary of the PQRST method for learning from textbooks

The five stages of PQRST	Student activity	Effect that PQRST has
Preview	Skim read a chapter paying attention to headings and sub-headings. Carefully read any introductory or summary sections	Induces student to organise the chapter and their thoughts about the topic it covers.
Question	Carefully read headings and sub-headings, turning them into questions.	Prepares the student to seek out specific information. Acts as an Advanced Organiser.

Read	Carefully read each section of the chapter, looking for answers to the questions developed in stage two.	Induces students to elaborate the material whilst encoding it.
Self-recitation	Attempt to recall the information read by reciting the main points either sub-vocally or vocally.	Induces the student to practice recall of the material.
Test	At the end of the chapter, attempt to recall the main points and how they relate to each other.	Induces further elaboration, practice of recall and rewards student via a sense of achievement.

METACOGNITION OR LEARNING ABOUT LEARNING: THE SPELT APPROACH

There are a number of different approaches to developing strategies for learning how to learn (see Lefrancois, 1997), but they all share the same basic idea: if we know how we learn, then we can improve our ability to learn. We shall look at just one example, Mulcahy *et al.'s* (1986) **Strategies for Effective Learning/Thinking (SPELT)**.

• **Table 5.8:** Summary of the SPELT approach to metacognition

Aims	To make students increasingly aware of their own cognitive processes and achieve metacognitive empowerment.
	To develop active teacher participation in identifying and discovering cognitive strategies and methods for teaching them.
	To ultimately develop autonomous learners who know how to learn and are in control of their learning.
Range of learning/ thinking strategies that form SPELT	General problem-solving, mathematical skills, reading skills, memory techniques, mood-setting strategies, comprehension monitoring, organisational strategies and so on.
Implementation: Phase one	Students taught above strategies by trained teachers using formal teaching style.

| Phase two | Students practice the use of and begin to evaluate the cognitive strategies learned in phase one. The teaching style is now informal with the teacher acting as facilitator. |
| Phase three | Students encouraged and supported in developing new cognitive strategies and evaluating their effectiveness. Informal, student-centred teaching. |

Designed for use with all students, from those with learning difficulties through to gifted students, SPELT is a learning/thinking instructional programme that focuses on the process of learning. Table 5.8 summarises the main characteristics of the SPELT approach to learning about learning.

Lefrancois (1997) comments that during a three year evaluative project involving over nine hundred students, ranging from those with learning difficulties to gifted students, the SPELT programme showed very positive improvements in learning. It seemed to be particularly effective for students with learning difficulties and also improved awareness and use of cognitive strategies improved for all groups at all grades.

To sum up, there are a wide variety of teaching and learning styles, many of them variations on a theme. It should be a teacher's responsibility to vary their teaching style to suit the learning needs of their students and to make the most of the subject content and resources available. It should be the student's responsibility to develop a range of study skills that complement their learning style and allow them to get the best out of their educational career.

Section summary — **Improving learning effectiveness (study skills)**

In this section we considered how, since learning styles are not fixed, students could develop strategies or techniques for improving the effectiveness of their learning. These were:

- McCarthy's 4-MAT System, which focuses on four components of learning: motivation, concept development, practice and application
- the PQRST method of learning effectively from textbooks. This involves the student in Previewing, Questioning, Reading, Self-recitation, and Testing themselves
- the SPELT approach that aims to develop Strategies for Effective Learning/Thinking, and is a metacognitive approach. In contrast with the other two study skills, this is concerned with learning *how* to learn, rather than a direct method of learning as such.

KEY TERMS

Curry's onion model: instructional preference; informational processing style; cognitive personality style; Myers-Briggs types indicators; Grasha's six learning styles: independent; dependent; competitive; collaborative; avoidant; participant; individual differences: learning orientation; formal–informal; high initiative–low initiative; approaches to studying Inventory (ASI); reliability; validity; McCarthy's 4-MAT system; the PQRST method; strategies for effective learning/thinking (SPELT).

EXERCISES

- Using the PQRST method, see how much you can learn about the next topic you are going to do on psychology and education *before* you start it in class!
- Try to identify which learning style(s) you use, and which teaching styles you experience. Do they vary from subject to subject? Do you think that changing your learning style is possible, desirable, or more trouble than it's worth?

SAMPLE EXAM QUESTIONS

1 (a) Describe one learning and/or teaching style.
  (b) Discuss the strengths and weaknesses of this learning and/or teaching style.

2 (a) Outline one method of measuring learning and/or teaching styles.
   (b) Evaluate the reliability and validity of measuring learning and/or teaching styles.

3 (a) Describe learning and teaching styles.
   (b) Evaluate learning and teaching styles.
   (c) Giving reasons for your answer, suggest how an understanding of learning styles can improve educational performance.

Further reading

Lefrancois, G. R. (1994) *Psychology for Teaching* (8th ed). Belmont, CA: Wadsworth.
Gives a good account of learning styles

Fontana, D. (1995) *Psychology for Teachers* (3rd ed). Leicester/Basingstoke: Macmillan/BPS Books.
The chapter on 'teacher personality, teacher characteristics, and teacher stress' gives a useful alternative view on teaching styles.

Websites

http://www.ed.gov/databases/ERIC_Digests/
United States Government Education Department official website. Provides summaries of research into all aspects of education.

http://chiron.valdosta.edu/whuitt/files/4matonweb.html
An article by William G. Huitt on McCarthy's 4-MAT system. Also contains links to the *Readings in Psychology* and *Educational Psychology Interactive* websites.

http://www2.ncsu.edu/unity/lockers/users/f/felder/public/Papers/LS-Prism.htm
A very readable article on learning styles. Gives a brief overview of four different models, how to use them in education and how to make teaching accessible to all types of learning styles.

http://web.indstate.edu/ctl/styles/learning.html
A useful article about the use of technology in relation to learning styles. Part of the Indiana State University Centre for Teaching and Learning website. Has a wide range of interesting material related to psychology and education.

Motivation and educational performance

Introduction

'Why?'

Of all the questions we ask of others and ourselves, perhaps this is the most important in understanding human behaviour. Why do some students work their socks off, whilst others couldn't give a monkey's? Why do some seem to have no problems meeting deadlines whilst others treat deadlines like buses … they turn up when they want to! The answer to all these sorts of questions lies in what we call motivation, the thing that makes us do whatever it is that we do.

This chapter will examine the following areas:

- definitions, types and theories of motivation, focusing on three main approaches:
  - ○ physiological approach: arousal and motivation
  - ○ cognitive approach: visualisation and motivational traits
  - ○ humanistic approach: Maslow's Hierarchy of Needs
- improving motivation, which will largely be integrated into the above section, rather than being considered separately
- motivation issues: attribution theory and learned helplessness.

Definitions, types and theories of motivation

DEFINITIONS OF MOTIVATION

Despite the differences of their conceptions of human behaviour, each of the three psychological approaches referred to above shares a common factor when it comes to defining **motivation**. That is, they all classify motivation as a *need* of some sort. In other words, they share the idea that we possess some deep-seated urges that force us to behave in the ways that we do.

Rubin and McNeil (1983, quoted in Gross, 1996, p.96), for example, define motives as those causes that ' … energise, direct and sustain a person's behaviour (including hunger, thirst, sex and curiosity)'. This definition has obvious links to all three approaches, with the first three examples of behaviour being physiological, curiosity being a cognitive behaviour and the humanistic perspective considering that, whilst we all share these motives the way that we behave in response to them is uniquely individual.

Similarly, Dweck's (1986) definition of motives as the cause of all our goal-directed activity can also be related to each of the three approaches. Why do we raid the fridge in the middle of the night? To satisfy our hunger. Why is a three-year-old's favourite word 'Why?'? Because they want to find out as much about the world around them as they possibly can. Why do comedians risk rejection every time they go on stage? Because making people laugh is the purpose of their life.

What we need to consider in this chapter, is *why* students learn and *why* some have a greater hunger for knowledge and learning than others.

PHYSIOLOGICAL APPROACHES TO MOTIVATION

The **physiological approach** to motivation focuses mainly on the basic survival needs that we have from birth. If we are hungry or thirsty, then we are motivated to reduce these needs by seeking out food and drink. Whilst this approach is important in understanding human behaviour in general, it is of relatively little value in explaining what motivates some students to study more than others.

While it is difficult to concentrate fully on any task if our stomach is rumbling with hunger pangs, the *survival motives approach*, as this has been termed, has little to offer the world of education. One physiological concept that is an important influence on learning, however, is that of arousal.

arousal and motivation

Lefrancois (1997) suggests that **arousal** is both a psychological and a physiological concept. The psychological aspect is concerned with the degree of alertness or attentiveness we display. The physiological aspect consists of the changes in heart rate, blood pressure, respiration and brainwave activity which underpin the different levels of alertness that we experience. Arousal is linked to motivation in two ways. According to the **Yerkes-Dodson Law**, for every task we undertake – and this includes educational tasks such as reading, writing essays or taking exams – there is a level of arousal at which performance will be at its optimum. This is shown in Figure 6.1.

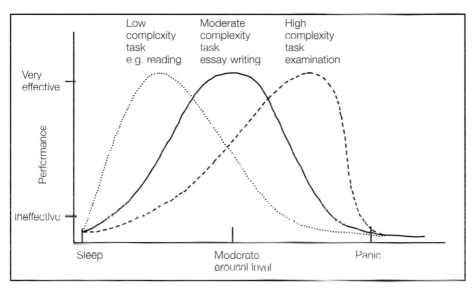

Figure 6.1. The Yerkes Dodson Law showing the relationship between arousal level and task performance for tasks of differing complexity (based on Lefrancois, 1997)

From the diagram we can see that when arousal is very low (when we are asleep), our performance at various tasks is not very effective. As we become more aroused, so our performance improves, until we reach the point of optimal performance. However, if our arousal level continues to climb, then our performance of the task will begin to decline.

As individuals, we behave in ways which attempt to keep our level of arousal as close to that needed for optimum task performance as possible. If we find something boring, for example, we may daydream, thus increasing our level of arousal, and helping us to drift back to the task at hand. Conversely, if we are over-aroused, we may do something to reduce the level of arousal, such as doodling on an exam paper to reduce the feeling of panic when we find that our mind has gone blank! In this way, the levels of arousal we experience within the classroom can affect our educational performance in both a positive and a negative way.

COGNITIVE APPROACHES TO MOTIVATION

Cognitive approaches to motivation are concerned with what and how we think about our behaviour and the planning that we put into achieving our goals. One cognitive approach to motivation is that of visualisation, whilst a second approach looks at motivational traits.

visualisation and motivational traits

According to Kagan and Lang (1978), we are capable of forming **cognitive representations** (i.e. thoughts, wishes, desires) of future events and it is this ability to foresee the future that is motivation. We have the ability to work out what we want to happen and can then direct our behaviour towards achieving that goal. Alternatively, we may be motivated by the difference in our current unsatisfactory reality and the probability that the future will be more satisfactory for us.

For us to motivate ourselves successfully, however, we must be able to visualise the desired outcome, or *see the future as we would like it to be, before it happens*. Thus, in much the same way as Linford Christie saw himself breaking the finish tape before anyone else at the start of a 100m race, so a student needs to visualise themselves actually handing the completed work to the teacher if they are to meet the set deadline.

Kagan and Lang further propose that visualisation achieves its effects through the operation of one or more of six major needs or desires and that teachers who are aware of these can plan their lessons to build on these desires to motivate their students. This approach is summarised in Table 6.1.

• **Table 6.1:** Kagan and Lang's major motives and examples of how teachers can utilise these in the classroom

Major motive or desire	Examples of what a teacher can do to allow these desires to be met and thus motivate students
Desire for approval from significant others	Establish an atmosphere in which both effort and quality work is seen as desirable by all
Desire to identify with others	Establish a relationship which fosters identification, by being a suitable role model ... prepared for every lesson, happy in their work, etc.
Desire for mastery	Set tasks that are achievable, but only after effort. Too easy tasks are as unmotivating as too difficult ones.
Desire to resolve uncertainty	Build up problem solving skills and set appropriate problems as part of class work
Desire for control, power and status	Encourage mutual respect, negotiate rather than impose deadlines for work completion (whenever possible)
Desire to vent hostility .	Be willing to accept criticism from students when it is warranted

That some of these factors do indeed motivate students has been shown in a study carried out on 944 Israeli science students by Ricardo Trumper (1995).

Trumper's questionnaire was designed to measure four **motivational traits** or characteristic ways of motivating oneself: achievement (broadly equivalent to Kagan and Lang's desire for mastery), curiosity (desire to resolve uncertainty), sociability (approval from significant others) and conscientiousness (perhaps a component of the desire for approval from others?). He found that 48 per cent of the students were motivated by a single trait (with 21 per cent identifying sociability as being the most important for them), whilst a further 29 per cent of the students were motivated by a combination of two traits. The remaining students stated that they were motivated equally by either three (15 per cent) or all four (8 per cent) of the factors measured. So what are the implications of this study for teaching?

Trumper cites Kempa and Diaz's (1990) claim that students whose primary motivational trait is sociability prefer group work and discovery-based learning rather than formal teaching, individual work and being individually tested, whilst Johnson and Johnson (1975) point out that co-operative working tends to result in a higher level of achievement. Given this, Trumper suggests that, at least in the first two or three years of secondary school, science should be taught in much the same way as it is at primary school level with students having the 'opportunity to exercise their own imagination and perform their own enquiries' (Trumper, 1995, p.513).

humanistic approaches to motivation

The **humanistic approach** to motivation focuses on what Csikszentmihalyi and Nakamura (1989) refer to as **intrinsic motivations**; those goals chosen by the individual that allow them to respond to curiosity and, to some extent, exercise free will over how they behave. Intrinsic motivations are in direct contrast to **extrinsic motivations**, which are the reinforcements we receive from others for our behaviour.

The pioneer of this approach was Abraham Maslow who proposed that humans have a dual needs system that can be arranged in a hierarchical fashion. At the bottom of the **hierarchy of needs** (1954) are four sets of basic or deficiency needs, which motivate us to gain something we lack. At the top are three sets of meta-needs or growth needs, which motivate us to become more than we are at present, as shown in Figure 6.2.

Maslow maintained that the needs at the lower levels had to be at least partially met before those in the level above it became important motivations for behaviour. This applies equally to the levels within the basic needs/meta-needs division as it does to that division itself. Thus when basics such as food and safety are threatened, the need for these is a far greater motivation of a person's behaviour than their need for belongingness and love, or the higher needs such as knowledge and appreciation of beauty.

Lefrancois quotes a survivor of the 1933 Ukrainian famine:

all you think about is food. It's your one, your only, your all-consuming thought. You have no sympathy for anyone else. A sister feels nothing for her brother; a brother feels nothing for his sister; parents don't feel anything for their children. You become like a hungry animal. That's what you're like when you're hungry. All human behaviour, all moral behaviour collapses (Lefrancois, 1994, p.277).

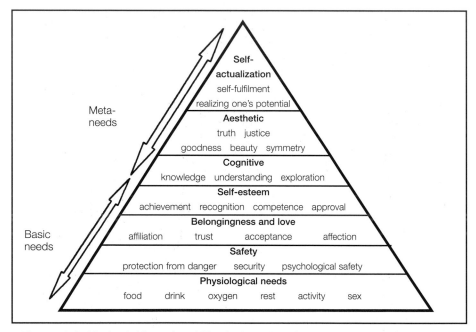

• **Figure 6.2:** Maslow's Hierarchy of Needs (based on Gross (1996) and Lefrancois (1997))

The experience of this survivor aptly sums up the powerful motivation that our basic survival needs can have on us. It is extremely unlikely that students in Britain today would ever have their basic needs threatened, but teachers should nevertheless ensure that school is a safe, warm, friendly place where every child is respected for who they are. This helps to create an appropriate environment in which, according to the humanistic approach, their cognitive and aesthetic needs will influence their behaviour, and thus motivate the students to achieve their potential as human beings.

It should be noted, however, that while passing exams can be the key to a good job which pays well and thus helps us satisfy our basic or deficiency needs, the meta-needs themselves, including the pursuit of knowledge, stem from a need to grow, to become truly human. As Maslow puts it: 'A musician must make music, an artist must paint, a poet must write, if he is to be ultimately at peace with himself. What a man can be, he *must* be' (Maslow, 1968, quoted in Gross, 1996, p.97). The fact that musicians or artists may become rich and famous as a result of selling their work is, from Maslow's point of view, secondary to their need to produce that artistic expression of their humanity in the first place. They are motivated to make music and paint not by profit, but by a driving need to explore the nature of their being. In other words, they are striving for **self-actualisation**: becoming the most complete human being that one can become.

Section summary

Definitions, types and theories of motivation

In this section we have seen that:

- motivation can be defined as the *cause* of human behaviour
- motives are concerned with the goal-directed behaviour we engage in, that goal being the satisfaction of needs
- the physiological approach focuses on basic, biological, survival needs, but offers one important concept in relation to educational motivation – that of *arousal*
- our level of arousal is related to our educational performance in what can be called an 'inverted U' fashion: too little and we become bored and perform poorly; too much and we become stressed and perform poorly; but with just the right amount we should perform optimally
- the cognitive approach of Kagan and Lang suggests that we will be better motivated if we can *visualise* a successful outcome to our endeavours
- the humanistic approach identifies two sets of motives: basic or deficiency needs and meta- or growth needs
- deficiency needs must be at least partially satisfied before growth needs influence our behaviour
- the humanistic approach also emphasises the distinction between extrinsic and intrinsic motivations and needs.

Theme Link – The free will versus determinism debate, and motivation

The free will versus determinism debate is centred on the question: Do we behave in the way that we do as the result of choices and decisions that we make as independent human beings, or are there factors outside of our control that lead us to behave in the way that we do?

The physiological approach to motivation comes down very firmly on the side of determinism. It argues that we are motivated to behave in the way that we do by the state of physiological arousal we are in. The higher the level of arousal (up to a point), the more motivated we are to do something. The lower the level of arousal, the less motivated we feel. Thus our behaviour is physiologically determined.

The cognitive approach also considers behaviour to be determined, but determined by how we process information, rather than the state of physiological arousal. Thus, whether we act and what we do in any given situation results from how we visualize the outcome of the behaviour (Kagan and Lang, 1978), the attributions that we make about our own behaviour (Weiner, 1984), and whether we are experiencing learned helplessness (Seligman and Maier, 1976). Whether we do experience learned helplessness (which is explained in detail on page 111) is determined by whether or not we perceive we have control over our environment.

In contrast to the deterministic outlook of the physiological and cognitive approaches, the humanistic perspective is most definitely on the side of free will. Although we are all motivated to achieve self-actualization, and although we all have the same needs to fulfil, the humanistic approach says that we are entirely free to choose our own path to realising our goals.

Improving motivation

You will be very well aware that some students are more motivated than others. You will also be able to recall lessons in which you worked extremely hard and others in which you just couldn't be bothered. In other words, there are inter-personal and intra-personal differences in levels of motivation. So what can teachers do to try to maximise the motivation of most of their students, most of the time?

From a physiological perspective, the teacher's task in the classroom is to maintain a level of arousal in the students that allows them to perform optimally. This can be achieved by carefully controlling the stimulation to which students are exposed. For example, by continually emphasizing the importance of tests, making tasks unrealistically difficult or prowling around the classroom staring at the students' work, the teacher can cause anxiety and lead to over-arousal. In order to reduce this, students may withdraw their attention and effort from the task – the exact opposite of what the teacher wants (Lefrancois, 1997). By providing the students with achievable goals, presenting information in an interesting and stimulating way, and using a variety of teaching styles, the teacher can go a long way towards ensuring that students are sufficiently aroused to perform optimally.

Kagan and Lang's cognitive perspective suggests that teachers ensure that students can visualise success at the task they are undertaking. To achieve this, teachers need to create a classroom environment that reflects and meets the major motives or desires that students possess. Ways in which this can be done are suggested in Table 6.1 earlier in this chapter.

From a humanistic point of view, the teacher can only influence the motivational level of a student so far. As already stated, the teacher needs to establish school as a safe, warm, friendly place so that the basic needs of safety, love and belongingness are met. The provision of wholesome, adequate, student-friendly meals also help to ensure that physiological needs are met. The teacher is then in a position to support the student in their pursuit of higher, aesthetic and cognitive needs. Some of the information provided in the section on humanistic applications to learning in Chapter 4 may also be relevant to the motivation of students. It is worth looking back at this section with this in mind.

Improving motivation

Section summary

In this section we have seen that students' levels of motivation can be increased by:

- maintaining a sufficient level of arousal to produce optimum performance
- using a variety of teaching styles and tasks
- setting tasks that are achievable, but still require effort
- supporting the students in their development of problem-solving skills
- ensuring the school environment is one that values the student as an individual and supports them in their pursuit of their meta-needs.

Motivation issues

ATTRIBUTION THEORY

Attribution theory is the 'explanation and evaluation of behaviour, both the behaviour of others and our own' (Georgiou, 1999, p.410) and Weiner (1984) suggests that attributions may be classified on three dimensions: locus, stability and controllability.

The concept of locus, or **locus of control** as it was termed by Rotter (1966) who first proposed it, is concerned with whether or not we perceive ourselves as being in control of our destiny. If we do, we have an *internal* locus. If other things like luck, fate, and so on determine what happens to us we have an *external* locus.

Stability is concerned with the fluctuation or otherwise over time of the factors that affect our behaviour. For example, luck is an unstable attribution, because luck can change from good to bad, but our ability to perform a certain task is more or less stable, after we have reached a certain level of skill.

Controllability is related to our perception of how much influence or control we have over those factors that affect our behaviour. You can control how much effort you put into revising, but you cannot control how difficult or easy the exam papers are going to be.

In addition, it has been shown that we make different attributions depending on whether the outcome of the behaviour has positive or negative consequences for us. The relationship between outcomes and Weiner's dimensions of attributions is summarised in Table 6.2.

• **Table 6.2:** Dimensions and examples of attributions made in relation to positive and negative outcomes

Attribution dimension		Examples of attributions	
		Positive outcome (e.g. passing an exam)	Negative outcome (e.g. failing an exam)
Locus	Internal	I passed because I really worked hard at that.	I failed because I didn't revise enough.
	External	I was lucky there. Everything I'd revised came up.	Typical, the questions I'd revised for didn't come up!
Stability	Stable	I've always been good at exams!!	I always go to pieces in exams … they just stress me out!
	Unstable	I worked out the right topics to revise.	The examiner set a really hard paper this year.
Controllability	Controllable	It was all down to my careful planning of revision.	I failed because I spent too much time revising my other subjects.
	Uncontrollable	Somebody up there likes me!	Why does everything work against me? Why can't I do anything right?

It should also be noted, of course, that these dimensions of attributions are themselves interconnected. It is possible to make internal, stable, controllable attributions (I passed the exam because I revised thoroughly, I'm good at the subject and I drew up essay plans for all the possible questions), external, unstable, uncontrollable attributions, (I passed because the teacher made us work really hard on our essay writing, the questions were easier than last year and I guess I must have written what the examiner wanted to read!), or any combination in between.

Probably the most important area of research into attribution theory with regards to education is understanding the types of reasons students give for their failure. These may suggest strategies that can be developed to assist students in achieving far greater success than they have so far. Central to this approach is the concept of learned helplessness, and it is to this that we now turn.

LEARNED HELPLESSNESS

The concept of **learned helplessness** was first developed by Seligman and Maier (1967). They showed that once dogs had been placed in an inescapable traumatic situation they subsequently gave up trying to escape from a later, similar, but this time escapable, situation. That is, once the dogs had experienced the helplessness of the first situation, they were affected and acted helpless in the second. Learned helplessness also applies to people in 'any situation where people think that they have no control over events. It does not matter whether there is a solution to their predicament or not, as long as they perceive the situation as hopeless then they will cease to find a way out' (Niven, 1989, p.141). In other words they have developed learned helplessness.

Learned helplessness in students may arise from the habitual use of undesirable attributions about failure. For instance, if a student failing an exam attributes this to lack of revision, then they are in control as they can revise harder for the re-sit. If, however, they attribute their failure solely to lack of ability then there is little they can do to correct the situation, and they will therefore perceive themselves as doomed to failure. Consequently, they give up trying and passively accept the idea that they lack the ability to succeed.

Dweck et al. (1978) have shown that one source of these undesirable attributions in students lies in the quantity and type of feedback students are given about their work. They also show that there are gender differences in the type and amount of feedback given and in students' responses to feedback, with girls more likely to develop feelings of helplessness than boys.

In an observational study measuring whether positive or negative, behaviour or work-related, intellectual (quality) or non-intellectual (e.g. neatness) feedback was given to fourth and fifth grade pupils, they found that, whilst there was little difference in the total amount of feedback given to boys and girls, girls tended to receive a significantly lower proportion of positive feedback and a higher proportion of negative feedback about the quality of their work compared to boys.

A subsequent experiment required children to solve firstly a set of solvable anagrams, then a set of unsolvable anagrams and they were finally given three attempts at solving a set of problems that they were never allowed to finish and which they were told that they had not done very well on. The children were then asked to select one of three reasons for their failure at the final task. During the anagram-solving tasks the children had been given the same sort of gender-related failure feedback that had been observed in the classroom observational study conducted by Dweck *et al*.

The results showed that the girls were more likely to attribute their failure on the final tests to a lack of ability, whereas the boys generally attributed it to a lack of effort or the fussiness of the experimenter. The conclusion that can be drawn from these studies is that if the majority of negative feedback given (particularly to girls) focuses on the quality of the work produced, then feelings of hopelessness and learned helplessness are more likely to result.

Section summary   **Motivation issues**

In this final section to this chapter on motivation we considered two issues: attribution theory and learned helplessness. The following points were considered:

- attribution theory is concerned with the explanations that we give for our own and others behaviour
- Weiner (1984) classifies attributions on three dimensions, each with two components: locus (internal/external), stability (stable/unstable) and controllability (controllable/uncontrollable)
- any individual explanation for behaviour can exist in one of many combinations of the two components of each of these dimensions
- learned helplessness is the state of believing that we have no control over what is happening to us, and that whatever we do will not affect the outcome of what we are going through
- there is evidence (Dweck *et al*., 1978) that learned helplessness in students can arise from the quantity and type of feedback they are given by teachers.

KEY TERMS

physiological approach; arousal; Yerkes-Dodson Law; cognitive approach; visualisation; motivational trait; mastery; control; cognitive representations; locus of control; stability; controllability; humanistic approach: Maslow's hierarchy of needs; self-actualisation; intrinsic and extrinsic motivations; attribution theory; learned helplessness

EXERCISES

- List five or six reasons why you are still at school or college. Are they intrinsic or extrinsic motivators?
- Imagine you are a teacher and your students have just failed a mock exam. How would you motivate them to improve on their performance for the real exam in a couple of months time?
- Keep a diary for a week recording the time(s) of day when you feel that you are alert and raring to go and when you feel that you are working well. Do they coincide? What does this say about arousal, motivation and performance?

SAMPLE EXAM QUESTIONS

1 (a) Describe one theory of motivation.
   (b) Discuss the strengths and weaknesses of this theory.

2 (a) Outline cognitive theories of motivation.
   (b) Compare and contrast the cognitive approach to motivation with that of one other psychological perspective.

3 (a) Describe theories of motivation in education.
   (b) Evaluate theories of motivation in education.
   (c) Giving reasons for your answer, suggest how a teacher
        could motivate students who are working at a lower level
        than they are capable of.

Further reading

Atkinson, R. L., Atkinson, R. C., Smith, E. E. & Bem, D. J. (1993) *Introduction to Psychology* (11th ed). Fort Worth, TX: Harcourt Brace Jovanovitch.
Provides a good introduction to the main psychological theories of motivation.

Lefrancois, G. R. (1994) *Psychology for Teaching* (8th ed). Belmont, CA: Wadsworth.
A very good chapter on motivation, with some useful case studies.

Websites

http://www.etln.org.uk/page37.html
The website for the Effective Teaching and Learning network. Contains an article on motivation and lots of other useful information.

http://www.garysturt.free.online.co.uk/edutime.htm
This site is provided by a teacher of OCR Psychology and contains information on most areas of the specification. Well worth bookmarking!

Disruptive behaviour in school

seven

Introduction

Being able to identify, correct and, even better, prevent, the disruption of learning caused by the inappropriate behaviour of some students is obviously of great importance to teachers. Failure to do so also has implications for students, both those who are being disruptive and those 'innocent bystanders', the remainder of the class, who are not being taught whilst the teacher is dealing with the disruptive pupil(s).

One definition of **disruptive behaviour** is that it is 'behaviour that proves unacceptable to the teacher' (Fontana, 1995, p.354). Whilst this may seem a rather simplistic definition, it emphasises the fact that it is teachers who decide what behaviours are or are not disruptive of the learning they are attempting to facilitate in the classroom.

It is important to bear in mind, however, that disruptive behaviour is just one aspect of classroom dynamics and should always be seen in that context. Relatively few students deliberately set out to disrupt lessons and a great deal of disruptive behaviour arises out of other factors, such as the students' lack of interest in the topic being taught, or a failure of the teacher to enthuse the students about the topic. Nevertheless, the issue of classroom control is probably the most anxiety-inducing one facing teachers today (Fontana, 1995).

This does not mean that disruptive behaviour is rampant throughout the education system, however. Although reports of physical attacks on teachers are increasingly seen in the headlines, it is important to realise that the majority of disruptive behaviours are of a petty nature, such as incessant chatter between students. Additionally, what one teacher may find disruptive another may not.

This chapter, then, examines the following areas:

- types, explanations and effects of disruptive behaviour
- causes and effects of one disruptive behaviour
- preventive and corrective strategies for dealing with disruptive behaviour.

Types, explanations and effects of disruptive behaviours

TYPES OF DISRUPTIVE BEHAVIOURS

Fontana's definition of disruptive, or, as he terms it, problem behaviour, quoted in the introduction highlights a major problem with defining this area of school life. Consider Tables 7.1 and 7.2. These show, firstly, that types of disruptive behaviour change over time and culture, as indeed do the methods used to discipline unruly students! They also serve to highlight the point made previously that the vast majority of disruptive behaviours are, in themselves, relatively minor.

• **Table 7.1:** Types of disruptive behaviours and their corresponding punishments in an American high school in 1848 (based on Fontana, 1994, and Lefrancois, 1997)

DISRUPTIVE BEHAVIOUR	PUNISHMENT
Misbehaving to girls	10 lashes
Drinking liquor	8 lashes
Swearing	8 lashes
Doing mischief about the place	7 lashes
Lying	7 lashes
Fighting	5 lashes
Playing cards	4 lashes
Boys and girls playing together	4 lashes
Wrestling	4 lashes
Quarrelling	4 lashes
Neglecting to bow when going home	2 lashes
Having long fingernails	2 lashes
Blotting one's copybook	2 lashes
For every word not recalled when given a list to learn by heart	1 lash

In addition to these relatively minor types of disruptive behaviours that almost any student is capable of displaying, there are other types such as attention deficit hyperactivity disorder (ADHD), which may be the result of some underlying psycho-physiological disorder. The next section looks at possible causes and effects of some of the more common minor disruptive behaviours (such as those listed in Table 7.2) and ADHD is considered later as an example of a specific disruptive behaviour.

• **Table 7.2:** Types and frequency of disruptive behaviour reported in the Elton Report into discipline in schools in England and Wales in 1989 (based on Fontana, 1994, and Lefrancois, 1997)

DISRUPTIVE BEHAVIOUR	FREQUENCY OF OCCURRENCE IN LESSONS (PER CENT)	
	At least weekly	At least daily
Talking out of turn	97	53
Idleness or work avoidance	87	25
Hindering other pupils	86	26
Unpunctuality	82	17
Unnecessary noise	77	25
Breaking school rules	68	17
Out-of-seat behaviour	62	14
Verbal abuse of other pupils	62	10
General rowdiness	61	10
Impertinence	58	10
Physical aggression to other pupils	42	6
Verbal abuse of teacher	15	1
Physical destructiveness	14	1
Physical aggression towards teacher	1.7	0

It is worth pointing out here that some researchers also consider disorders such as autism and dyslexia to be disruptive behaviours, in that they certainly disrupt the learning of the individual sufferer and may be disruptive for others in the same class as a student with these conditions. In this book these disorders are included in the chapter on special educational needs, as it could be argued that the nature of these disorders and the responses they require from the education system are of a different order to those behaviours described in Table 7.2. This does not mean, however, that they should not be considered as examples of specific disruptive behaviours.

EXPLANATIONS FOR AND EFFECTS OF DISRUPTIVE BEHAVIOURS

One possible explanation for minor disruptive behaviours may well lie with the teacher. If a teacher does not manage the classroom environment effectively, they may inadvertently not only invoke, but also reinforce disruptive behaviour.

Lefrancois (1997) points out that classrooms are very complex environments. Some may contain a mix of ethnic groups, ability ranges, language skills and so on, whilst others are much more homogeneous. All classes, however, share four common features as summarised in Table 7.3.

• **Table 7.3:** The four common features of classrooms

Feature	Explanation
Multidimensionality	Classrooms contain a variety of different personalities, with different backgrounds, abilities and goals.
Simultaneity	Classroom events never happen one at a time; there is always more than one thing going on.
Immediacy	Some events require immediate attention from the teacher, who has to respond and make decisions rapidly if the classroom activity is not to be disrupted too much.
Unpredictability	Given the other three features, classroom events are unpredictable.

It would seem then that a teacher has an almost overwhelming task in front of them when they step into the classroom, and the way that they respond, or fail to respond to this complex situation may well produce responses from the students which the teacher considers to be disruptive.

Fontana suggests that teachers first need to ask themselves why they consider behaviour to be disruptive. He asks 'Is it a sign of their own insecurity that they regard a child's attempt at humour as a threat to their authority? Have they perhaps been over-reacting to the group who tend to chatter over their work? Have they been setting unrealistically high standards and then become frustrated and angry when they are not achieved?' (Fontana, 1995, p.354). If they have, then it is very likely that they have actually caused resentment or confusion amongst their students by 'taking offence when none was meant, by tending to nag children, by being over-serious or apparently unfair, by being over-dignified and pompous, by expecting too much, by being inconsistent' (Fontana, 1995, p.355).

It may be that such teachers are lacking, to a greater or lesser degree, what Kounin (1970, cited in Cotton, 1990) identified as the five characteristics of effective classroom management behaviour. These are summarised in Table 7.4.

• **Table 7.4:** Kounin's five characteristics of effective classroom management behaviour (based on Cotton, 1990)

Characteristic	Explanation
Withitness	Awareness of what is going on everywhere in the classroom; being able to interpret and act upon verbal and non-verbal cues.
Overlapping	'Multi tasking' – ability to do several things at once.
Smoothness and momentum	Pursuing the objectives of a lesson in a brisk but smooth manner whilst taking disruptions in one's stride.
Group-alerting	Using random questioning of individuals to make them accountable for learning by realising that they could be next. Also bringing an element of unpredictability to teaching so that students' attention is focused and maintained.
Stimulating 'seatwork'	Variety is needed to prevent students becoming bored with the 'same old stuff'; tasks set should be challenging, but must allow for a high degree of success if progress is to be made. Teacher feedback is crucial to the success of their students.

Lefrancois (1997) gives a very good example of this effective classroom management in his recounting of a teacher who, whilst reading Dickens to a sixth grade class, acknowledges one pupil's urgent need to go to the toilet and intercepts a note being passed from one pupil to another, without once stopping reading in a captivating, attention-grabbing way. Thus the lack of effective classroom management on behalf of the teacher may provoke disruptive behaviour from the students, whilst its possession is a very good preventive technique.

If teachers are a possible cause of disruptive behaviour, then the other possible cause must be related to the students themselves. As seen in the chapter on motivation, Maslow argues that one of the essential needs of human beings is that of having our existence recognised by others. When we are very young, gaining and holding someone else's attention has obvious survival value – how else would a baby get food? We have also seen in the chapter on perspectives that we can learn behaviours through reinforcement. Most of us learn very quickly as young children that simply asking for attention usually achieves it and so our appropriate behaviour is reinforced. This is probably down to the simple fact that most of us are brought up in caring, loving environments, and thus we behave in a socially acceptable way.

Others, however, are not so fortunate. If the only way a child can gain attention from its parents is by displaying inappropriate behaviour, then it will do so. For such a child, even the negative attention that its inappropriate behaviour brings about is better than no attention at all. According to Riding and Craig (1999, p.312) 'lack of love and recognition in childhood result in a feeling of insecurity, low self-worth and potentially of a difficulty in interpersonal relationships'.

Loeber and Stouthamer-Loeber (1986), considering the results of British, American and Scandinavian studies on family factors and behaviour, concluded that the main influence on disruptive behaviour was neglect of children by their parents, and the related lack of involvement and effective relationship they had with them. This situation is further compounded by inconsistent, harsh discipline administered in an unloving manner. Riding and Craig also concluded that the absence of parental love and recognition and a consistent, reasonable disciplinary regime is likely to result in disruptive behaviour being exhibited. If a teacher responds to a child's disruptive behaviour in a similar way to its parents, then the feelings of insecurity and low self-worth will become intensified.

Thus two possible explanations for disruptive behaviours in the classroom are the lack of effective management by the teacher and parental neglect for the child resulting in the learning of inappropriate behaviours.

Section summary   **Types, explanations and effects of disruptive behaviours**
In this section we have seen that:

- there is a wide variety of disruptive behaviours
- they can vary from the relatively minor disruption of talking out of turn to the more serious disruption of physically assaulting a teacher
- some psychologists/educators would also classify some learning difficulties as disruptive behaviours
- what constitutes disruptive behaviour changes over time
- there are individual differences in teachers' tolerance for disruptive behaviour
- one possible explanation for disruptive behaviours is the teacher's lack of, or inappropriate use of, classroom management skills
- another possible explanation lies in the student's family circumstances.

The use of perspectives as an evaluation issue is very useful as it allows us to understand the often unspoken assumptions that are made when applications of psychology are suggested. Disruptive behaviours can, in one way or another, be related to each of the five traditional perspectives in psychology.

Psychologists such as Eysenck would argue that the degree of extroversion and introversion that we show is determined by the underlying level of arousal in the part of the central nervous system known as the ascending reticular activating system. Thus the possibility that an introverted teacher has a lower threshold for disruptive behaviours than an extroverted one is, ultimately, a function of their biology.

Behaviourists would argue that disruptive behaviours, such as attention-seeking behaviour, are learned through the processes of operant conditioning and the observation and modelling that is social learning.

Cognitive psychology assumes that it is the way that we *process* information that determines our behaviour. This is very apparent in the cognitive behavioural approach to correcting disruptive behaviour described towards the end of this chapter. The basic premise is that, if the way that we *think* is changed, then our behaviour will change to reflect this.

Both the schoolwide and the classroom approaches to preventing disruptive behaviour described below contain elements of the humanistic perspective. They emphasise the needs of students and the importance of teachers regarding their students as individuals with their own understanding of the world. They also focus on the need for any disciplinary programme to target the *behaviour*, not the person, for fear of jeopardising their self-esteem.

Finally, the pattern of behaviour that the student shows towards the teacher may reflect the interactions that the child has with her/his parents. The psychodynamic perspective would argue that the teacher represents a symbol of authority, similar to the parents, and the child, unable to express any form of hostility at home for fear of punishment, may displace that hostility onto the teacher.

Causes and effects of one disruptive behaviour: Attention deficit hyperactivity disorder

Attention deficit hyperactivity disorder (ADHD) can also occur without the hyperactive element, in which case it is known as *attention deficit disorder* (ADD). AD(H)D:

is a neurological condition which is probably genetic in origin, where the sufferer has a very reduced ability to maintain attention without distraction, has little control of doing or saying something due to impulsivity and lack of appropriate forethought, and, where hyperactivity is also present, no control over the amount of physical activity appropriate to the situation (SENR, 2001, p.1).

Rosenhan and Seligman (1989) point out that AD(H)D is about five times more common in boys than girls, and its overall prevalence is between six and seven per cent. Although the severity of the disorder can diminish over time, it is never completely overcome and, although there are no known cases of adults developing the disorder, there are adults who are diagnosed with it following a failure to diagnose or a misdiagnosis during childhood.

Lefrancois (1994) states that it is assessed on the child showing at least eight characteristics that are displayed for at least six months, before the age of seven. Table 7.5 details the characteristic behaviours of someone with AD(H)D. It should also be noted that as well as displaying these characteristics, they must be displayed more frequently and severely than most other children of the same age.

• **Table 7.5:** The characteristics of attention deficit hyperactivity disorder (based on LeFrancois, 1994 and SENR, 2001)

Characteristics of AD(H)D
• fidgeting/restlessness
• difficulty remaining seated when required to
• easily distracted
• difficulty in turn-taking in games and group situations
• often blurts out answers to questions
• difficulty in following instructions
• difficulty at tasks requiring sustained attention
• often shifts from one incomplete activity to another
• difficulty in playing quietly
• often talks excessively
• interrupts others often
• often does not seem to listen
• often loses things
• often takes physical risks, without considering the consequences
• chronic procrastination

It is obvious from this table that the effects of AD(H)D are highly disruptive for the education of the sufferer. Inability to sustain attention, for example, will lead to great difficulty in acquiring the basic skills of reading and writing to anything other than a basic level. Other characteristics, such as problems with turn-taking and impulsivity, will disrupt the learning of wider social skills that are also important in developing academic ability. Additionally, the behaviour manifested by AD(H)D sufferers can be disruptive for the rest of the class. The definition of AD(H)D given above states that it is probably a genetic disorder, but what is it precisely that causes this disorder? Research has focused on two related but opposing ideas. One school of thought says that the cause of AD(H)D lies in a chronically over-aroused central nervous system resulting in the continual switching of attention. Other theorists suggest that, in fact, the opposite is true – chronic under-arousal results in the inability to maintain attention. The fact that AD(H)D is currently most successfully controlled by the use of stimulant drugs such as Ritalin suggests that the latter explanation is the most plausible. At the moment, though, the precise cause of this disorder has not yet been identified.

Causes and effects of one disruptive behaviour: Attention deficit hyperactivity disorder

Section summary

In this section we have seen that:

- AD(H)D is a childhood disorder which persists into adulthood
- it is characterised by the possession of at least eight characteristics
- for at least six months to a greater extent and severity than non-sufferers
- it is very disruptive of learning
- it has been suggested that either chronic over-arousal or chronic under-arousal may be the cause
- it is currently best controlled with stimulant drugs, such as Ritalin.

Preventive and corrective strategies for dealing with disruptive behaviours

The first point here is that although both preventive and corrective strategies may, to some degree, rest on the same underlying psychological principles, their focus in relation to disruptive behaviours is very different. Preventive strategies are aimed at stopping disruptive behaviours *before they even start* and can be developed at both the school and classroom level. Corrective strategies are concerned with *responding* to the student who has misbehaved in a way that will lessen the likelihood of that misbehaviour recurring.

PREVENTIVE STRATEGIES

school level

At the school level, **preventive strategies** for dealing with disruptive behaviours are concerned with establishing rules, procedures and routines which ensure that students know what behaviours are and are not appropriate and, equally important, the consequences of inappropriate behaviours. Most research in this area has been conducted by comparing schools with good disciplinary practices with those that have poor disciplinary practices in order to identify the critical differences between them.

In her review of 54 research studies conducted in Australia, England, New Zealand, Norway, Scotland and the United States on this topic, Cotton (1990) proposes that schools that operate effective preventive discipline share the seven components outlined in Table 7.6.

• **Table 7.6:** The components of schoolwide preventive discipline practices (based on Cotton, 1990)

Component	Explanation
Commitment	All staff must be committed to establishing and maintaining appropriate student behaviour as an essential precondition of learning.
High behavioural expectations	Staff share and communicate high expectations for appropriate student behaviour.
Clear and broad-based rules	Rules, punishments and procedures for dealing with disruptive behaviour are developed with input from students, who thus feel a sense of ownership and belongingness. The rules are clearly written, widely disseminated, and both students and staff understand what is and is not acceptable.
Warm school climate	A warm social climate, characterised by a concern for students as individuals. All staff take an interest in the personal goals, achievements and problems of students, and support them in their academic and extracurricular activities.
A visible, supportive headteacher	A headteacher who is very visible in the hallways and classrooms, talking informally with staff and students, speaking to them by name, and expressing an interest in their activities.

| Delegation of discipline authority to teachers | Whilst the headteacher maintains responsibility for dealing with serious problems, teachers are held responsible by the head for handling routine classroom discipline. The head arranges for staff development around this issue as needed. |
| Close ties with the local communities. | A high level of parental involvement in school functions and activities, with a high flow of information about its goals and activities from the school to the parents. |

We can see that schools which operate preventive strategies are those that have clear expectations about how students should behave and ensure that students, staff, and parents are aware of those expectations. In addition – and as a way of balancing what may at first appear to be a very formal, autocratic approach – these schools espouse the humanistic ideas of respect for and interest in the individual student.

As Short puts it 'research on well-disciplined schools indicates that a student-centred environment, incorporating teacher–student problem-solving activities, as well as activities to promote student self-esteem and belongingness is more effective in reducing behavior problems than punishment' (Short, 1988, p.3, cited in Cotton, 1990, p.4).

In addition to, or possibly instead of, preventive discipline strategies at the school level, teachers may also need to call upon preventive strategies within the classroom, and it is these that we will now consider.

classroom level

As already suggested in the section on causes of disruptive behaviour, the key to effective prevention of disruptive behaviour at the classroom level is classroom management. One preventive strategy is for teachers to be given appropriate training in the development of Kounin's five characteristics of classroom management, described in Table 7.4 earlier. In addition, Cotton (1990) cites a wide range of research which underscores Kounin's findings about the nature of effective classroom management and its relation to disruptive behaviour. Cotton reaches the conclusion that there are seven major, empirically validated, behaviours that comprise effective classroom management and these are outlined in Table 7.7.

• **Table 7.7:** Components of effective classroom management that act as preventive strategies for disruptive behaviour (based on Cotton, 1990)

- Holding and communicating high expectations for student learning and behaviour. Through the personal warmth and encouragement they express to students and the classroom requirements they establish, effective manager/teachers make sure that students know they are expected to learn well and behave appropriately.
- Clearly establishing and teaching classroom rules and procedures. Effective managers teach behavioural rules and classroom routines in much the same way as they teach subject content. These are reviewed at the beginning of the school year and periodically thereafter. Classroom rules are displayed in primary school classrooms.
- Clearly stating consequences and their relation to student behaviour. Effective managers are careful to explain the connection between students' misbehaviours and teacher-imposed punishments. This connection too, is taught and reviewed as needed.
- Enforcing classroom rules promptly, consistently and fairly. Effective managers respond quickly to disruptive behaviour, respond in the same way at different times and impose the same punishment regardless of gender, ethnicity or ability.
- Sharing with students the responsibility for classroom management. Effective managers work to inspire in their students a sense of belonging and self-discipline, rather than seeing discipline as being externally imposed.
- Maintaining a brisk pace for instruction and making smooth transitions between activities. Effective managers keep things moving in their classrooms, which increases learning as well as reducing the likelihood of misbehaving.
- Monitoring classroom activities and providing feedback and reinforcement. Effective managers observe and comment on student behaviour, and they reinforce appropriate behaviour through the use of verbal, symbolic and tangible rewards.

CORRECTIVE STRATEGIES

Even the best-prepared, most effective manager or teacher will, from time to time, find themselves faced with disruptive behaviour and be called upon to deal with it. This means that they will have to utilise **corrective strategies**, which can be defined as ways of dealing with disruptive behaviour *after* it has occurred. Lefrancois argues that in any disciplinary situation there are two paramount considerations. 'The first is that the individual not be harmed – that whatever the teacher does is done in the best interests of the student, with full consideration for that person's self-esteem and humanity. The second is that the disciplinary measures invoked should be applied in the interests of the entire group' (Lefrancois, 1997, p.303).

Given these considerations, it is relatively easy for a teacher to get it wrong; nevertheless, there is a range of corrective strategies available for teachers to call on as and when the need arises. Broadly speaking, these can be classified as those deriving from the behavioural perspective and those based on the cognitive approach. One example of each approach will be considered here.

behaviour modification techniques

Based on the principles of operant conditioning and the concept of behaviour shaping, the goal of **behaviour modification** techniques is to change or eliminate the disruptive behaviour and replace it with more appropriate, desired behaviour. Table 7.8, based on the work of Presland (1989), cited in Lefrancois (1997), outlines the main stages of a behaviour modification approach to disruptive behaviour with an individual student.

Here is an example of how this might be put into practice. A teacher has a student who spends most of every lesson talking to those sitting beside him. The teacher has to ask him to be quiet at least a dozen times a lesson. In recognising this, the teacher has identified and measured the disruptive behaviour. The teacher then realises that his talking starts when she directs questions to students sitting on the other side of the classroom, and that the only time she talks to this student is to tell him to be quiet.

• **Table 7.8:** Stages in a behaviour modification programme (based on Presland, 1989, cited in Lefrancois, 1997)

Stages of behaviour modification	Action taken by teacher
1. Defining the problem.	Draw up a list of behaviours that are too frequent (speaking out of turn) and too infrequent (volunteering answers to questions). The student might be involved in this step.
2. Measuring the problem.	Determine how serious the problem is, perhaps by counting occurrences.
3. Determining antecedents and consequences.	Identify what happens before the behaviour, and its consequences. In other words, identify what triggers the behaviour and what reinforces it.
4. Deciding whether and how to change antecedents and consequences.	Consider whether there are existing consequences that serve to reinforce a too-frequent behaviour. Identify new consequences that might reinforce an infrequent behaviour.

5. Planning and implementing the intervention.	Devise a programme to modify the behaviour in question through the use of selective reinforcement.
6. Following up.	Evaluate the effectiveness of the programme with the student and determine whether or not additional or different intervention is desirable.

Thus her attention is reinforcing the talkativeness, whilst the times when he is attentive to what is going on in class are going unrewarded. The teacher then determines that she will pay more attention to him, by asking him questions early on in the lesson, and attempt to ignore the talking to others as much as she can. The aim of this is to reinforce his attentiveness and extinguish his talkativeness through withdrawal of reinforcement.

While this may work in theory, the biggest problem with the behaviour modification approach is that the teacher is not the only person who can provide reinforcement in the classroom. The attention from fellow students may be far more important to the student than that received from the teacher! Nevertheless, Cotton, in her review of schoolwide and classroom discipline reports that 'many researchers (Brophy, 1983, 1986; Cobb and Richards, 1983; Cotton, 1988; Crouch et al., 1985; Docking, 1982; McNamara et al., 1987; Moskowitz and Hayman, 1976) have identified reinforcement (verbal, symbolic or tangible) as effective in improving the classroom conduct of misbehaving students' (Cotton, 1990, p.7).

cognitive behaviour modification

This approach uses the principles of behaviour modification and allies them with cognitive strategies so that, not only is the student's behaviour changed, but so is the way they think about what they are doing. Meichenbaum (1977, cited in Lefrancois, 1997) argues that very often the effects of the consequences of our behaviour may be more closely related to our ability to imagine and anticipate those outcomes than to the outcomes themselves. Thus, **cognitive behaviour modification** attempts to address not only the maladaptive behaviour, but also the maladaptive cognitions that lead to the behaviour in the first place.

• **Table 7.9:** Meichenbaum's self-instructional training

Stages of self-instructional training	Description
1. Cognitive modelling	Teacher performs task while talking out loud about what they are doing, why they are doing it, and why they have discarded other options. This focuses the students' attention on the task and what needs to be done to complete it. It also allows them to realise that mistakes can be corrected, and that a slower methodical approach leads to success.
2. Co-working	The student is asked to repeat the task and the talking out loud, but the teacher guides them as they do so. The student experiences success at the task for the first time.
3. Imitation	The student repeats the task while self-instructing aloud, but without guidance from the teacher.
4. Sub-vocal performance with lip movement	The student repeats the task, but this time repeats the self-instruction in thought while moving their lips.
5. Sub-vocal performance without lip movement	The student repeats the task again, but this time only sub-vocal instruction is used and no lip-movement occurs.

One example of a cognitive behaviour modification strategy is that devised by Meichenbaum and Goodman (1971, cited in Gross, 1996) known as **self-instructional training** (SIT). This programme was devised in an attempt to reduce the disruption in learning caused by the impulsivity and hyperactivity displayed by a group of children.

SIT basically supports children in developing their understanding of what needs to be done to succeed at a task whilst, at the same time, encouraging them to pay more attention to what they are doing, to take their time and think about the next move they need to make. The five stages of SIT are detailed in Table 7.9. In Meichenbaum and Goodman's original 1971 study the first task given to the children was a line-drawing task. In four subsequent sessions, increasingly complex and demanding tasks were used, and the children seemed to become more reflective and less impulsive in their approach to these tasks and subsequent work. They also made significantly fewer errors (Lefrancois, 1997).

To sum up, teachers can call upon a range of schoolwide and classroom management techniques or strategies to attempt to prevent disruptive behaviours from occurring in the first place. However, if they do occur, there is also a wide range of corrective strategies available to them, behaviour modification and self-instructional training being just two examples.

Section summary   **Preventive and corrective strategies for dealing with disruptive behaviours**

In this final section about disruptive behaviours we have seen that:

- preventive strategies are utilised to stop the disruption *before* it starts, whereas corrective strategies are concerned with changing the disruptive behaviour *after* it has been exhibited
- preventive strategies can be applied at both school and classroom levels
- school level strategies focus on the development and implementation of policies concerned with, for example, clearly setting out disciplinary procedures and establishing links with the local community
- classroom level strategies are based around classroom management techniques and include the establishment of a clear set of rules of behaviour and ensuring students are aware of the teacher's expectations about their behaviour
- corrective strategies are based on behavioural and/or cognitive principles
- behaviour modification techniques use the principles of operant conditioning to shape the disruptive behaviour to a more desirable one
- cognitive behavioural strategies, such as self-instructional training, attempt to change not only the behaviour, but also the thinking that accompanies it.

KEY TERMS

disruptive behaviour
preventive strategies
corrective strategies
behaviour modification
cognitive behaviour modification
self-instructional training

EXERCISES

- Keep a diary of how your behaviour may be considered disruptive during your psychology lessons.
- Find out what policies your school or college has for dealing with disruptive behaviours.
- Discuss the likely causes and effects of disruptive behaviours with your classmates.

SAMPLE EXAM QUESTIONS

1 (a) Describe different types of disruptive behaviour.
   (b) Discuss possible causes of one of these behaviours.

2 (a) Describe types of disruptive behaviour and their effect.
   (b) Compare and contrast behaviourist applications to disruptive behaviours with applications from other perspectives.

3 (a) Describe types and causes of disruptive behaviours.
   (b) Evaluate types and causes of disruptive behaviours.
   (c) Giving reasons for your answer, suggest how teachers can prevent disruption from arising in their classroom.

Further reading

Lefrancois, G. R. (1994) *Psychology for Teaching* (8th ed). Belmont, CA: Wadsworth.
An insightful account of disruptive behaviours, despite its American slant.
Fontana, D. (1995) *Psychology for Teachers* (3rd ed). Leicester: Macmillan/BPS Books.
Another insightful account, but look under the heading of *behaviour problems*!

Websites

http://auseinet.flinders.edu.au/stream3/s3projects-Behaviou.html
The website of the Australian Network for Promotion, Prevention and Early Intervention for Mental Health. This page contains an article on disruptive behaviour, but there is plenty of other relevant information as well.

http://www.cfc-efc.ca/docs/00000883.htm
The website for Child and Family Canada. This page contains an article on disruptive behaviour.

Design and layout of educational environments

eight

Introduction

> A classroom, like a church auditorium, is rarely seen as being anything other than that which it is. No one entering either place is likely to think that he is in a living room, or a grocery store, or a train station. Even if he entered at midnight ... he would have no difficulty understanding what was *supposed* to go on there. Even devoid of people, a church is still a church and a classroom, a classroom (Jackson, in Moon and Shelton Mayes, 1994, p.156).

This quotation from Jackson sums up the enduring effect that the classroom environment has on us. Even adults returning to learning after a break of decades find themselves remembering their schooldays as soon as they set foot in a classroom.

Based on this anecdotal evidence, it would be easy to make the assumption that all classrooms are identical, but they are not. As you sit in your classroom, take a look around you. What colour are the walls? Are there any pictures or posters on the walls and if so what are they of and where did they come from? What furniture is there in the room? How is it laid out? Who decided where the desks and chairs should be and why? Blackboard or whiteboard? There are lots of other similar questions you might consider.

Why are these things important? Well, if the behaviourists are to be believed then our behaviour is determined by the environment in which it occurs. It follows then that academic behaviour, in terms of the amount and quality of work that students produce, will also be open to environmental influences.

Environmental psychology is the branch of psychology that is concerned with how the physical world affects human behaviour. Environmental psychologists carry out research into the effects of things like the climate and weather, the built environment (e.g. housing), natural disasters and technological catastrophes. Organisational psychologists are concerned with examining and explaining how organisations such as places of work affect the way we behave. They conduct research into topics like work stress and job satisfaction, work conditions, leadership and management. Both environmental and organisational psychologists have shown that the way in which buildings are constructed and the way in which rooms within those buildings are designed and laid out can have profound effects on what happens in those rooms.

This chapter will examine the following areas:

- physical features of the classroom environment
- the effects that these have on educational performance and feelings
- creating better educational environments.

The effects that physical features of the classroom have on educational performance and feelings will be examined at the same time as we examine the feature itself, rather than looking at the effects in a separate section. The reason for this is simply that it is easier to understand the relationship between the feature and its effects if they are considered together.

Physical features of the classroom environment and their effects on educational performance and feelings

The **physical features** of the classroom environment include such things as lighting, noise, seating arrangements and so on. The physical features also include what are known as **aesthetic features**, such as the colour of the walls, posters and work presentations that adorn the walls. We will look at each of these in turn.

LIGHTING

Cave (1998) suggests that lighting is a complex factor to deal with – aspects such as the amount, type, colour, location of the light source, reflectiveness of surfaces such as walls, desks and ceiling must all be taken into consideration. Riggio (1990) states that increasing levels of illumination tend to be matched by improvements in performance, but a point is reached where this positive relationship begins to tail off. Indeed, if the light is increased too much, then it can prove to be a distraction and so lead to a decline in performance. This can be seen in Figure 8.1.

According to Sanders and McCormick (1987, cited in Riggio, 1990) the most important factor in determining when performance stops increasing with light levels is the amount of fine visual discrimination. This would suggest that subjects like Art, Textiles and Sciences, which can involve the need for highly detailed, small scale work, may be more susceptible to the effects of illumination than, say, Mathematics, English, or Psychology. The trick seems to be to find a balance between the amount of light and the task to be done. Generally speaking, an illumination level of about 500 lux (a standard measure of illuminance) would seem to be optimum for the type of tasks undertaken in the classroom.

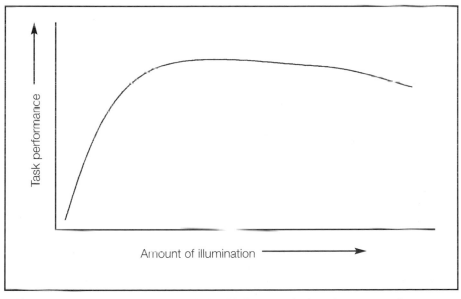

• **Figure 8.1:** Diagram showing the relationship between task performance and illumination

Another consideration in relation to lighting in classrooms is the energy efficiency of the lighting. Riggio (1990) points out that *fluorescent lighting* is both more energy efficient and has a more even light distribution pattern than incandescent bulbs – this accounts for their widespread use in schools. One annoying feature of fluorescent lighting, however, is its tendency to buzz, and as we shall see in the next section, noise levels can also affect performance.

NOISE

How many times have your parents told you to 'turn that noise down!' when you have been listening to your favourite CD while doing your homework (or not, as the case may be!)? Why is it that what *you* think is wonderful music, *they* perceive as noise, and more likely than not, vice versa? The answer probably lies in the commonly accepted definition of noise as some unwanted, distracting sound that interferes with task performance and is therefore a source of stress (Sarafino, 1998).

According to the (American) Environmental Protection Agency's 1974 review of research into the effects of noise on cognitive performance, noise may or may not negatively affect such performance. Factors such as the frequency, duration, pitch and loudness of the noise have to be taken into account. In addition, there are individual differences in responses and for some people noise may actually enhance their performance. After all, some of you are able to study to the sound of your CD player blasting out, whilst others of you prefer silence.

This anecdotal evidence is backed up by a study conducted in Belgrade by Belojevic, Slepcevic and Jakovljevic (2000). They found that introverted subjects had greater concentration problems and suffered fatigue far more frequently than extroverts when completing mental arithmetic tasks under noisy conditions (recorded traffic noise at 88 dB). The findings of the Environmental Protection Agency are summarised in Table 8.1.

• **Table 8.1:** Effects of noise on cognitive performance (adapted from Riggio, 1990)

- Noise does not generally have an adverse effect on performance unless it exceeds 90 decibels (equivalent to that of lorries and lawnmowers).
- Intermittent or unpredictable noises are more disruptive than steady, predictable noises.
- High-pitched noises interfere with performance more than low-pitched noises.
- Noise is more likely to reduce the accuracy of cognitive performance than to reduce the amount of work done.

Maxwell and Evans (2000), in a study involving 90 four- and five-year-old children, found that those being taught to read in a classroom where sound absorbent panels had been used to reduce noise levels scored higher on letter–number–word recognition tasks. They were also rated by their teachers as having a better understanding and use of language than those children who had been through the same classroom prior to the noise attenuation work being carried out.

These results are in line with the Environmental Protection Agency's conclusion about the relationship between noise and cognitive performance, as are Neill's (1982) findings that the use of carpeting to lessen reverberant noise increases educational talk between staff and children.

One of the findings of the Belojevic et al. (2000) study mentioned earlier, however, seemingly contradicts the claim that noise affects accuracy rather than amount of work. They found that there was no significant difference in the accuracy of work completed by their participants in the quiet and noisy conditions, and the extroverts performed significantly faster in the noisy condition compared with the quiet condition. Thus, it would seem that the general principles outlined by the Environmental Protection Agency need to be treated with a degree of caution. Equally, one should not forget the mediating effects of individual differences, such as personality type or learning style.

AESTHETIC FACTORS – COLOUR

Despite the fact that home designers are constantly telling us about the positive and negative effects of colours on our moods, there is surprisingly little research into this area in education. One study by Nancy Stone (2001), suggested that adult students showed a slightly more positive mood when performing reading and Maths comprehension tasks in a blue carrel compared to a red carrel. In addition, their performance at the reading task was significantly lower in the red environment. Whilst this evidence is limited, it nevertheless serves to make the point that consideration should be given to the colour that classroom walls are painted, as it may have an effect on students' academic performance.

SEATING ARRANGEMENTS

Marland (1975) suggests that the traditional placing of the teacher's desk at the front-centre of the classroom strikes a somewhat cold, impersonal note, despite the obvious advantage it has for monitoring student behaviour. He argues that serious consideration should be given to altering the arrangement of furniture in a classroom in order to foster a warmer and more friendly environment.

Lefrancois (1994) emphasises the point that creativity is enhanced and student discipline problems are lessened in a friendlier environment. Figure 8.2 shows four possible seating arrangements. It also shows that, even in classrooms where certain features (such as position of windows, doors, blackboard and storage space) are fixed, teachers are still able to manipulate the seating arrangement to match the learning objectives for their lessons and/or the teaching style they use.

The notion that simply altering the seating arrangements in a classroom can have a significant effect on students' performance is highlighted in a study by Bennett and Blundell (1983). In this study, two classes of 10- and 11-year-old children, matched in class size, age and sex distribution, were tested every two weeks for six weeks, on the quality and quantity of work produced in three areas, reading, language comprehension and Mathematics. In the first two weeks they were in their normal classroom groups, seated around tables, in the middle two weeks they were seated in rows, with two children per table. For the final two weeks they returned to their original groups around tables.

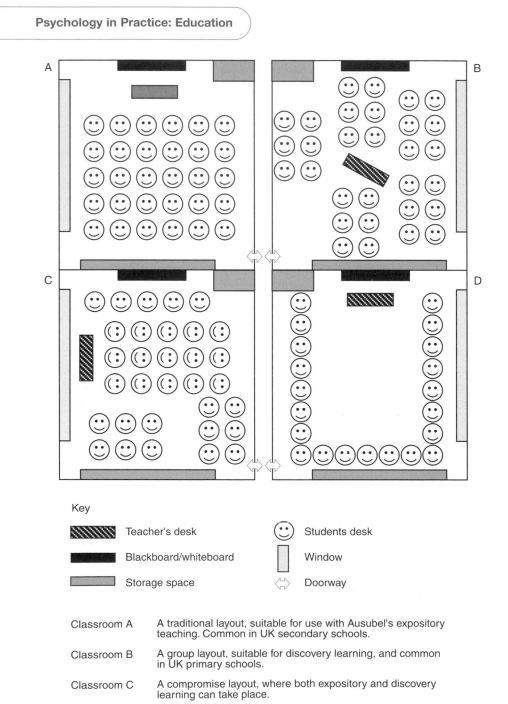

Key

Teacher's desk		Students desk	
Blackboard/whiteboard		Window	
Storage space		Doorway	

Classroom A   A traditional layout, suitable for use with Ausubel's expository teaching. Common in UK secondary schools.

Classroom B   A group layout, suitable for discovery learning, and common in UK primary schools.

Classroom C   A compromise layout, where both expository and discovery learning can take place.

Classroom D   A 'horseshoe' layout, suitable for expository teaching, but allowing more student interation than traditional layout. Common in further and higher education.

• **Figure 8.2:** Four possible ways of arranging seating and desks in a classroom with an indication of their suitability for different teaching styles

Overall, there was a significant increase in the *quantity* of work when the children were seated in rows, with a less marked decline when they returned to groups. There was an overall increase in the *quality* of work when the children were moved to rows, but this did not slide back to previous levels when they returned to their groups. 'In other words, quantity has not generally been achieved at the expense of quality' (Bennett and Blundell, 1983, p.103) when seating arrangements have been changed.

The authors of this study also note that, when interviewed after the study, teachers reported a noticeable improvement in behaviour when the students were seated in rows, followed by an increase in talking when they returned to their groups. Interestingly, despite some reservations about the row arrangement cutting down on the amount of available space, all the students stated that they preferred sitting facing the front of the class.

Linked to this forward-facing preference are Montello's (1988, cited in Cave, 1998) findings that pupils seated at the front of the class tend to be more participative and attentive than those seated towards the rear, although there is no significant difference in their achievement.

Effects of physical features of a classroom on educational performance   Section summary

In this section we have looked at theory and research that examines the effect of physical features of the classroom on educational performance. The following was discussed:

- lighting is an important factor that can improve or lower educational performance depending on how it is used
- the pitch, duration, predictability and volume of noise affected educational performance; there is also a relationship between noise and students' personality type
- there is some evidence that aesthetic factors such as the colour of the walls can affect mood and educational performance
- there is evidence that changing the seating arrangements of pupils from groups to rows results in a significant improvement in educational performance
- teachers are able to alter the seating arrangements to match the educational objectives of any lesson, and four main types are used: traditional, group, compromise and horseshoe.

Theme Link – Design and Layout of Educational Environments and Determinism

Determinism is the term given to the idea that human behaviour can be influenced, perhaps even caused, by factors over which we have no control. These factors may be physiological (physiological determinism) or environmental (environmental determinism).

Evidence such as that put forward by Neill (1982), Bennett and Blundell (1983), Sanders and McCormick (1987), Maxwell and Evans (2000) and Stone (2001) implies that educational performance and the mood of students is a direct result of the environment and, as such, is beyond their control. In order to improve educational performance, the teacher simply needs to manipulate the learning environment. In other words, educational performance is environmentally determined, a view very closely related to the behavioural approach to psychology.

The study by Belojevic *et al.* (2000), however, could be used to argue that the relationship between environment and educational performance is not quite this straightforward. Their finding that personality mediates this relationship suggests that educational performance is determined by an *interaction* between the environment and physiological factors (if we accept the argument that personality has a physiological basis, which itself is hotly debated). This would mean that educational performance is determined by two forces over which we exert little, if any, control.

Humanistic psychologists, however, would argue that educational performance is very much in the *control* of the individual. We are all free to work as hard or as little as we want, irrespective of the colour of the classroom walls, the seating arrangement chosen by the teacher, or any other environmental factors.

Creating better environmental conditions for learning

Having briefly considered the physical factors that affect the classroom environment and the effects they have on academic performance, it is now time to consider how the classroom environment can be improved in order for it to have the most beneficial effect on learning. It is important to point out that in designing a classroom, variables such as class-size, age-range, purpose, the subject(s) being taught in that room, the teaching styles of the teacher(s) and so on should all be taken into account.

Other variables, such as the nature of the institution, also play a part. For instance, a primary school teacher, who usually has her/his own classroom, has far more control over the classroom layout than a secondary or tertiary teacher who may have to share a multi-purpose room. In other words, there is no such thing as an ideal classroom, but nevertheless it is still an important aspect of education that needs to be carefully thought through.

* **Table 8.2:** Assessment of the classroom environment (from Mellard *et al.*, 2001)

ASPECT OF LEARNING ENVIRONMENT	YES	NO	N/A
Lighting is adequate for any activities that require visual work.			
Lighting can be adjusted for use with AV materials; students can still see all relevant materials.			
Visual environment is free of unnecessary distractions.			
Visual environment is appropriately stimulating to attention and learning.			
Seating is comfortable.			
Seating is arranged so that all students can view and access all necessary components of the learning environment.			
Shape and size of the room is appropriate for the type of teaching and learning that occurs.			
Location of the instructor in relation to all students is appropriate.			
Acoustics of the room allow all students to hear instructor, other students and audio when appropriate.			
Background noise is minimal or non-existent.			
Workspace is accessible to all students.			
Workspace allows each student to access all needed materials and tools.			
Temperature of the room is comfortable.			
All students can enter, exit and move about the room freely.			
Doorways into and out of the room are located in such a way that they allow for entry, exit and bypassing without distracting those inside.			
In an emergency situation, students with disabilities could exit safely.			
Other:			

Perhaps the starting point for any teacher is to carry out an **environmental assessment** of their classroom to decide what, if anything, needs modifying. This can either be done informally by simply drawing up a checklist of environmental factors, such as lighting, heating, décor or, more objectively, by using a classroom environment assessment schedule such as that devised by Mellard *et al.* (2001) and reproduced in Table 8.2.

The advantage of the assessment schedule over the informal approach is that it ensures that all aspects of the physical classroom environment are considered and it has a higher degree of validity and reliability. Having made the assessment, the teacher is then in a position to modify the environment accordingly. This may mean altering the lighting, seating arrangements, acoustic quality of the room via installation of acoustic panels, carpeting and so on. This assumes, of course, that the funds are available to make the desired modifications.

Wolery (1994, cited in NCREL, 2001) points out that additional factors have to be taken into account when designing a classroom in which students with special educational needs are to be taught alongside other students. These include keeping the arrangement of activity areas and seating constant if the child has a severe visual impairment, or re-orienting the child every time the layout is changed. Wheelchair access should be possible around all areas and work surfaces and students should be able to move around the classroom freely.

If teachers are given the time, resources, knowledge and support from fellow staff, headteacher, school governors and local education authority then there is little reason for classroom environments to be a barrier or a hindrance to learning in any way.

Section summary **Creating better learning environments**

In the final section of this chapter on design and layout of educational environments we have seen that:

- factors such as class-size, teaching style and subject(s) taught in the room have to be considered
- informal assessment of the educational environment is often undertaken by teachers
- formal assessment using an environmental checklist is more reliable and ensures that all the important aspects of the educational environment are taken into account.

KEY TERMS

environmental psychology
organisational psychology
physical factors
aesthetic factors
environmental assessment
learning environment

EXERCISES

- Try re-arranging the seating in your classroom and note any differences in behaviour and learning that occur. Rate each seating arrangement for its effectiveness. You may want to construct some sort of scale to do this.
- Try threading a needle under different lighting conditions. Under which condition did you perform this task the quickest? What are the implications of this for education?
- Cover the walls of a room in black paper, or any other single colour. (I suggest you get permission first, and use blu-tack rather than wallpaper paste!!) How does it make you feel? Does it affect your ability to concentrate on a task?

SAMPLE EXAM QUESTIONS

1 (a) Describe one physical factor of the classroom environment that has an effect on educational performance.
   (b) Discuss the effects that this physical factor has on educational performance.

2 (a) Describe factors in the classroom environment that have an effect on educational performance.
   (b) Evaluate factors in the classroom environment that have an effect on educational performance.

Dale, R., Ferguson, R. & Robinson, A. (Eds) (1988) *Frameworks for Teaching: Readings for the Intending Secondary Teacher*. London: Hodder & Stoughton.

Demie, F. (2001) Ethnic and Gender Differences in Educational Achievement and Implications for School Improvement Strategies, *Educational Research, 43* (1), 91–106.

Dessent, T. (1987) *Making the Ordinary School Special*. London: The Falmer Press.

Dweck, C.S., Davidson, W., Nelson, S. & Enna, B. (1978) I: Sex differences in learned helplessness: II: The contingencies of evaluative feedback in the classroom. III: An experimental analysis. *Developmental Psychology*, 14, 268–276.

Dweck, C. S. (1986) Motivational Processes Affecting Learning. *American Psychologist*, 41, 1040–1048.

Ewing, T. (2001) *Gender Differences Similar Across Racial/Ethnic Groups*. Educational Testing Service. http://www.ets.org/research

Felder, R. M. (1996) Matters of Style. *ASEE Prism, 6* (4), 18–23 or at: http://www2.ncsu.edu/unity/lockers/users/f/felder/public/Papers/LS-Prism.htm

Fontana, D. (1994) *Managing Classroom Behaviour* (2nd revised ed of *Classroom Control*). Leicester: BPS Books

Fontana, D. (1995) *Psychology for Teachers.* Basingstoke and Leicester: MacMillan/BPS Books.

Gipps, C. & Murphy, R. (1994) *A Fair Test? Assessment, Achievement and Equity.* Milton Keynes: Open University Press.

Gross, R. (1996) *Psychology: The Science of Mind and Behaviour* (3rd ed). London: Hodder & Stoughton.

Gould, S. J. (1981) *The Mismeasure of Man*. Harmondsworth: Penguin.

Jackson, P. (1994) *Life in Classrooms*. In B. Moon & A. Shelton Mayes *Teaching and Learning in the Secondary School*, London: Routledge.

Jordan, R. & Jones, G. (1999) *Meeting the Needs of Children with Autistic Spectrum Disorder*. London: David Fulton Publishers.

Lefrancois, G. R. (1994) *Psychology for Teaching* (8th ed). Belmont, CA: Wadsworth.

Maker, C. J. & Udall, A. J. (1985) *Giftedness and Disabilities*. ERIC EC Digest # E427. http://ericec.org/digests/e427.html

Maxwell, L. E. & Evans, G. W. (2000) The Effects of Noise on Pre-School Children's Pre-Reading Skills. *Journal of Environmental Psychology, 20*, 1, 91–97.

Mellard, D., Berry, G., Gilbert, M., Dunn, W., Lancaster, S. & Kurth, N. (2001) *Assessment of the Classroom Environment*. http://das.kurcl.org/iam/assessclass.html

Murphy, P. & Moon, B. (1989) *Developments in Learning and Assessment*. London: Hodder & Stoughton.

NCREL (North Central Regional Education Laboratory) (2001) *Designing the Classroom Environment*.
http://www.ncrel.org/sdrs/areas/issues/students/earlycld/ea41k24.htm

Neill, S. (1982) Experimental Alterations in Playroom Layout and Their Effect on Staff and Child Behaviour. *Educational Psychology, 2* (2), 103–119.

Nicholls, G. (1999) *Learning to Teach*. London: Kogan Page.

O'Connor, T. (1997) *Using Learning Styles to Adapt Technology for Higher Education*. http://web.indstate.edu/ctl/styles/learning.html

Powell, S. (ed) (2000) *Helping Children with Autism*. London: David Fulton Publishers.

Riggio, R. E. (1990) *Introduction to Industrial/Organizational Psychology*. London: Scott, Foresman/Little Brown.

Rosenhan, D. L. & Seligman, M. E. P. (1989) *Abnormal Psychology* (2nd ed). London/New York: Norton.

Rotter, J. B. (1966) *Generalized Expectancies for Internal Versus External Control of Reinforcement. Psychological Monographs, 30* (1), 1–26.

Rubin, Z. & McNeil, E. B. (1983) *The Psychology of Being Human* (3rd ed). London: Harper & Row.

Rudduck, J. & Gray, J. (2001) *Gender and Achievement: Recent Trends*.
http://www.standards.dfee.gov.uk/genderandachievement/data_1.2.1.html

SENR (Special Educational Needs Resources) (2001)
http://www.geocities.com/sen_resources/definitions.html

Scgroeder, C. C. (2001) *New Students –New Learning Styles*
http://www.virtualschool.edu/mon/Academia/KierseyLearningStyles.html

Scott Bauman, A. Bloomfield, A. & Roughton, L. (1997) *Becoming a Secondary School Teacher*. London: Hodder & Stoughton.

Selikowitz, M. (1998) *Dyslexia and Other Learning Difficulties: The Facts*. Oxford: Oxford University Press.

Shuttleworth, I. (1995) The Relationship between Social Deprivation, as Measured by Free School Meal Eligibility, and Educational Attainment at GCSE in Northern Ireland, *British Educational Research Journal, 21* (4), 487–504.

Solity, J. & Raybould, E. (1988) *A Teacher's Guide to Special Needs: A Positive response to the 1981 Education Act*. Milton Keynes: Open University Press.

Stapleton, M. (1993) *'New York, London, Paris, Munich, Everybody Talk About Pop Music' (M):Theorising Modern Popular Music From Adorno to Post Modernism*. Unpublished dissertation in partial submission for MA in Cultural and Textual Studies, University of Sunderland.

Stone, N. J. (2001) Designing Effective Study Environments, *Journal of Environmental Psychology*, Ideal First Articles.
http://www.idealibrary.com/links/doi/10.1006/jevp.2000.0193

Sukhnandan, I., Lee, B. & Kellerher, S. (2000) An Investigation into Gender Differences in Achievement Phase 2: School and Classroom Strategies. http://nfer.ac.uk/

Weiner, B. (1984) *Principles for a Theory of Student Motivation and Their Application within an Attributional Framework*. In Ames, C. & Ames, R. (1984) *Research on Motivation in Education: Student Motivation, 1*, 145–170.

Zimbardo, P. (1992) *Psychology and Life* (13th ed). New York: Harper Collins.

Index